HEALTHY
FOR YOU AND

Fiona Ford, Robert Fraser and ~~~~~~~~~~~ are respectively a dietitian, obstetrician, and nutritionist. They all work at the Centre for Pregnancy Nutrition based in the University Dept of Obstetrics and Gynaecology, Northern General Hospital, Sheffield.

HEALTHY EATING FOR YOU AND YOUR BABY

*A comprehensive guide
to what you should (and shouldn't) eat before,
during and after pregnancy*

FIONA FORD, ROBERT FRASER

AND

HILARY DIMOND

PAN BOOKS
LONDON, SYDNEY AND AUCKLAND

First published 1994 by Pan Books

an imprint of Macmillan Publishers Limited
Cavaye Place London SW10 9PG
and Basingstoke

Associated companies throughout the world

ISBN 0 330 33755 6

1 3 5 7 9 8 6 4 2

A CIP catalogue record for this book is available from
the British Library

Typeset by CentraCet Limited, Cambridge
Printed and bound in Great Britain by
Cox & Wyman Ltd, Reading, Berkshire

Contents

Acknowledgements

We would first like to thank Rosie Barnes, the Director of WellBeing, for her support for the Centre for Pregnancy Nutrition, and for writing the Foreword to this book. Vivienne Parry was instrumental in setting up the Helpline by arranging a WellBeing grant. This was funded from a donation to WellBeing from Tesco Stores PLC. We have also received financial support and encouragement from the Alumni Foundation of Sheffield University, through the Alumni Office, and in particular Elizabeth O'Brien.

We would also like to express our thanks to Rose Elliot for allowing us to use some of the vegetarian recipes from her book *Rose Elliot's Mother and Baby Book*.

Finally the Authors and Publishers would like to thank the Health Education Authority for kind permission to reproduce the 'Balance of Good Health' plate (page 80), for which they hold the copyright.

Foreword

by Rosie Barnes, director of WellBeing

Whilst it has always been recognized that it is important to eat well during pregnancy, it is only as a result of fairly recent research that it has been realized just how vital a healthy diet is, not only in the short term for the pregnant woman and her baby, but for her baby's future health. We now suspect that adult diseases such as heart problems, strokes and diabetes often have their origins in the eating patterns of a pregnant woman with major effect not only for her baby but for that child in later life. Research findings indicate that even the most healthy diet and exercise regime pursued by any individual cannot negate the effects of nutritional deprivation during their mother's pregnancy.

We now also know that even before pregnancy diet is extremely important. It has been demonstrated that folic acid at around the time of conception is very important in minimizing the chances of the baby developing neural tube defects, the most commonly known of which is spina bifida.

WellBeing, the health research charity for women and babies, formerly Birthright, has been interested in this area for many years. We have funded many research projects on all aspects of nutrition in pregnancy. We have also funded the telephone helpline for anxious women or those seeking more information at the Centre for Pregnancy Nutrition in Sheffield.

Every piece of research conducted in this area seems to indicate an even greater importance of nutrition in pregnancy than had ever been imagined. It may be that preventative medicine should in future be concentrated on the pregnant women because in many medical areas once the baby is born the pattern for its future health may have already been laid down.

WellBeing is currently funding three major research projects in this area. At the University of Southampton we are funding a project to study how maternal iron deficiency can affect the growth of the baby between 18 weeks of pregnancy and birth. Possibly the most exciting piece of research is also at Southampton, where a team will be studying fetal growth and adult disease amongst a sample of people, now around fifty years of age, whose mothers were starved whilst pregnant as part of the German embargo of Western Holland in the war. Finally, a team at the University of Sheffield are studying calcium uptake in pregnancy to be able to advise pregnant women of the precise need for this important mineral in their diet.

As more and more women begin to realize the importance of their diet, not just to produce a healthy baby but to give their child the best chance throughout its life, they will naturally seek information in this vital area. I am delighted that this helpful and detailed book has been written by a team who have been actively concerned about nutrition in pregnancy for so many years. I am sure women will find it invaluable and it will be important to teenage girls, young women and pregnant mothers, empowering them to contribute not only to the growth but to the long-term health of their babies by giving them the best possible start in life.

Introduction

This book has arisen from the recent developments relating to diet and pregnancy which have improved our knowledge in this area. It has also arisen from our increasing awareness at the Centre for Pregnancy Nutrition, where we run the 'Eating for Pregnancy Helpline', of the concerns and anxieties of both pregnant women and those planning a pregnancy in relation to their diet. These include worries that the information they receive is neither accurate nor up to date, and complaints that they feel very restricted in what they can and cannot eat.

Our intention in writing this book is to be informative without being alarmist. All recommendations are based on reliable evidence from scientific surveys and experiments. Where ideas are unproven or mere speculation this will be made clear. Generally speaking, advice on diet or lifestyle changes will be given only where the evidence is conclusive. It is potentially harmful to follow ideas which have not been tested and proved, however sensible and logical they may sound.

The following chapters discuss why it is important that women should examine their diet if they are planning to become pregnant. They also explain how your body changes and what can influence the growth of your baby. They give detailed advice, too, about the foods and nutrients that you should include in your diet, plus information about food safety and how to avoid infection from salmonella, listeria and toxoplasmosis as well as general food hygiene guidelines.

Common pregnancy problems such as sickness, taste changes, dietary cravings and aversions, anaemia, constipation and pre-eclampsia are also discussed, as are breast and bottle feeding.

We hope you find this book both enjoyable and informative and that by following the advice you increase the prospect of your pregnancy being healthy and your baby being born in the best possible condition.

'Eating for Pregnancy Helpline'

based in the Centre for Pregnancy Nutrition, Sheffield

The 'Eating for Pregnancy Helpline' service was established in September 1991 and is available to members of the public, the media, and fellow scientists and health professionals. It disseminates information concerning nutrition during the preconception period, pregnancy and lactation. It was initiated because of increasing concern among pregnant women and those planning a pregnancy about their diet and its impact on the developing baby.

During the first 30 months of its existence almost 3,000 queries have been received, 72 per cent from the general public, 20 per cent from health professionals, whilst 4 per cent were media enquiries and 3 per cent were enquiries from students and consumer organizations. The proportion of enquiries from professional colleagues has shown a gradual increase from 8 per cent in the first 12 months to its present figure of 20 per cent. This is very encouraging because midwives, health visitors, dietitians and general practitioners can disseminate the information to a wider audience.

A variety of publications and posters is sent out to enquirers, most of which are produced by the Centre for Pregnancy Nutrition, but Department of Health and Health Education Authority publications are also supplied.

The most common queries received concern food safety, vegetarianism, vitamin and mineral supplementation, weight gain, nausea and vomiting. An increasing number of enquiries are from women planning a pregnancy.

The aim of this book is to provide the information that the

helpline has shown women want – but after reading it, if you still have any concerns call:

Eating for Pregnancy Helpline
Tel 0114–2424084 (Mon–Fri and 24-hr answerphone)
Fax 0114–2617584

CHAPTER ONE

Planning Ahead

IS IT IMPORTANT TO TRY TO PLAN FOR YOUR BABY?

In the real world, the majority of pregnancies are not consciously planned and many couples are concerned that things might go wrong because of this. By and large the evidence is reassuring. It seems that human fertilization takes place only when it is likely to lead to a successful outcome. Women who are seriously undernourished, for instance, fail to produce eggs from their ovaries and miss their monthly periods. Women who are seriously overweight also often have difficulty conceiving.

There are some good reasons, however, to plan ahead for a pregnancy and the following sections explain why. If you have just read this and you are already pregnant please do not become alarmed. It is never too late to benefit from improving your diet and altering your lifestyle so that you, your partner and your baby lead a healthier life.

DIETARY CONSIDERATIONS WHEN PLANNING A PREGNANCY

Your body is composed of cells and tissues made from the nutrient building blocks you obtain from food. If you have a 'full store cupboard' before pregnancy then your baby is not likely to run short of any essential nutrients. The two nutrients which are particularly important to look at before pregnancy are folate and iron.

Folate/folic acid

Folate, a vitamin often referred to as folic acid, is particulary important around the time of conception and during early pregnancy. Recent research has shown that the number of babies born with serious handicapping conditions such as spina bifida (or neural tube defects) is reduced when women increase their folate intake before conception and for the first three months of pregnancy. Folate is present in many foods (see Table 11 in Appendix 2). Its richest sources are leafy green vegetables (especially Brussels sprouts, spinach and broccoli), potatoes, oranges, yeast extract and fortified bread and breakfast cereals. Frozen vegetables often have as much folate as fresh, though food preparation can cause large losses of folate (see page 82 for more information).

All women who are planning a pregnancy are now advised to take a daily supplement of 400 mcg (micrograms) folic acid prior to conception and throughout the first three months of pregnancy, and to have a folate-rich diet (see Table 11 in Appendix 2). These 400-mcg supplements are not available on prescription, but are easily obtainable from pharmacies and health food shops (current brands available include Solgar, Health Aid and Boots). Women who have had a previous pregnancy where the baby was affected by spina bifida or a similar neural tube defect are now advised to take a much higher dosage folic acid supplement of 5 mg (milligrams) to reduce the risk of recurrence and this is available on prescription.

Eventually it may be discovered which women are most at risk of having a baby with spina bifida. Until this time, however, it seems prudent for all women planning a pregnancy to take folate supplements, particularly as there are no known side effects at this level of supplementation. However, if you are already pregnant and have not been taking supplements or having a folate-rich diet, it is important to remember that neural tube defects such as spina bifida are a very rare occurrence and most women are screened during pregnancy to detect whether their baby is affected.

Iron

Many women require iron supplementation during pregnancy because their body stores of this mineral are not sufficient for the increased demands for this nutrient. Try to ensure that your iron intake is adequate before pregnancy (see Appendix 1, page 159 and Table 17 in Appendix 2 for good sources of iron). In the most recent UK national dietary intake survey the majority of women were not achieving the Department of Health's recommended daily intake for iron.

OTHER PRE-PREGNANCY LIFESTYLE CHANGES

Smoking

The evidence that smoking is harmful in pregnancy is now beyond dispute. Women who smoke or who are affected by passively smoking have more miscarriages and are three times more likely to have a baby born with a low birthweight. In addition, smoking can affect your fertility – it takes longer on average for smokers to conceive than non-smokers, so the best time to give up smoking is before becoming pregnant. Giving up smoking before pregnancy and allowing your body to adjust to this may also prevent you from putting on excess weight during pregnancy. Evidence shows that women who give up smoking during pregnancy are more likely to put on too much weight and to have difficulty losing it after the birth. However, benefits to the developing baby are seen whenever the decision to give up smoking is made. Consider giving up together if your partner also smokes. If you cannot give up smoking whilst pregnant, remember that any cigarette you *don't* light helps the baby's growth and development.

Exercise

It is known that women who exercise for pleasure or as part of their employment and replace a large part of their body fat with muscular tissue may stop producing an egg every month and lose a regular menstrual cycle. Studies have suggested that about 2 or 3 per cent of normal women have problems producing an egg every month or having a regular menstrual cycle, whereas amongst cross-country and marathon runners sometimes up to a quarter of participants in these sports do not have periods regularly. Amongst professional ballet dancers as many as four out of ten may not be having regular periods.

Obviously training of an intensity which stops the production of eggs would be a major problem if the woman was also trying to get pregnant, and to some extent heavy athletic demands and conception do not go well together. Anyone who finds themselves in this position should be reassured by the knowledge that a slight reduction in exercise coupled with an attempt to increase body weight, by about 5 per cent, will usually result in a return to regular menstrual periods. If this alteration in exercise and diet does not have the desired effect over a period of six to twelve months then consultation with a doctor would be wise.

Medicines and drugs

If you have a medical condition for which you take regular medication – especially for conditions such as diabetes or epilepsy – it would be prudent to tell your doctor that you are planning a pregnancy before stopping contraception. A change of treatment may reduce the risk of having a damaged or handicapped baby.

WOMEN WHO PARTICULARLY NEED TO PLAN THEIR PREGNANCIES CAREFULLY

Women with an inappropriate body weight

Having an appropriate body weight means that you have a better chance of having a successful and healthy pregnancy. In order to tell if your body weight is too high or too low you must also take into account your height. The most reliable method of doing this uses a formula known as the Body Mass Index (BMI). The shaded bands on the following charts were created using this weight and height formula. Weigh yourself without clothes and, using the chart, take a straight line up from your weight in stones (or kilograms), and a line across from your height (without shoes). The point where the two lines meet will fall into a shade-coded weight band which will indicate how your weight rates. The chart does not apply if you are already pregnant. Having an appropriate body weight means that you have a better chance of having a successful and healthy pregnancy.

It must be strongly emphasized that when a reference is made to overweight or underweight women, it actually means those women who are clinically overweight or underweight as shown on the charts. Many women are not happy with their body size and shape and perceive themselves to be too fat or too thin but they actually fall into the normal weight for height category. It is important to check on the graphs before jumping to conclusions about your own body type.

An example of the different weight bands for a woman who is 1 m 63 cm/5 ft 4 in is given below

Weight Category	Weight Range		Band
	(kgs)	(st lbs)	
Underweight	37.8kg– 45.5kg	6st 0lb– 7st 3lb	1
Normal weight	46.0kg– 64.5kg	7st 4lb–10st 2lb	2
Overweight	70.0kg– 78.0kg	10st 3lb–12st 4lb	3
Fat	78.5kg–104.0kg	12st 5lb–16st 5lb	4
Very fat	104.5kg and above	16st 6lb and above	5

Are you the correct weight for your height ?

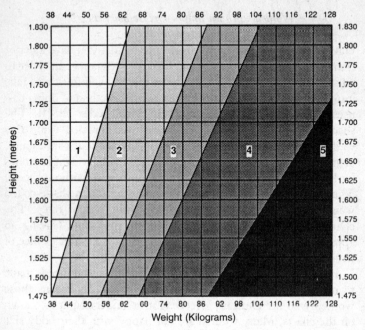

Are you the correct weight for your height ?

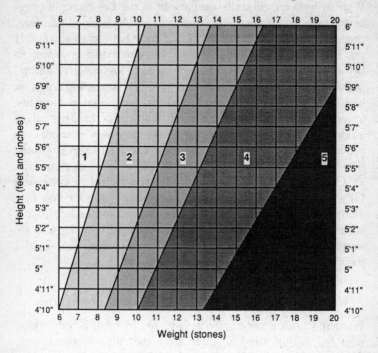

WOMEN WHO ARE OVERWEIGHT BEFORE CONCEIVING

This group includes women who are within bands 3, 4 and 5. Women who are clinically overweight at the beginning of pregnancy have an increased risk of developing high blood pressure, pregnancy diabetes and of delivering their baby prematurely. If you are overweight it is a good time to try to reduce your weight before you try to conceive. Sensible weight loss involves following the advice on pages 84–86 and 91–93 about cutting down on high-fat and high-sugar foods and checking that the energy (calories) that you get from food follow the healthy eating guidelines. This makes sure that all the necessary nutrients are provided by your diet. There are many excellent support groups that women can attend to get help to lose weight (see Appendix 3). Or you can talk to the practice nurse attached to your local GP's surgery who may feel it is appropriate to refer you to a dietitian. Don't forget that it takes a long time to lose excess weight and a miracle won't happen overnight; ½–1 kg (1–2 lb) weight loss per week is appropriate and at that rate, over 6 months, the weight loss will total 18 kg (3 st).

WOMEN WHO ARE UNDERWEIGHT BEFORE CONCEIVING

Women who are very underweight, or, in other words, those who fall within band 1, often have difficulty in conceiving. Women who are moderately underweight when they conceive run an increased risk of having a low birthweight baby. Low birthweight babies have more illness during the newborn period and can suffer from handicaps.

Women who are clinically underweight include those who are not eating enough, who are undertaking excessive physical exercise, who do not absorb their food properly (malabsorption syndrome) and those with eating disorders.

It is difficult to suddenly increase food intake, so you should start slowly by increasing slightly the size of your meals and then including inbetween meal snacks. If by increasing your food intake your weight is not rising, talk to your GP, who may then refer you to a dietitian for more detailed advice, and the possible use of nutritional supplements.

If you should become pregnant whilst underweight, do not worry about this. As long as you are able to eat a good general diet, there will be plenty of nourishment available for the baby.

Women with closely spaced pregnancies

The ideal interval between pregnancies is not known, although those of 2–4 years are seen in women who breastfeed exclusively and who do not use contraception, so this is probably what nature intended. Two or three years between births allows the body to recover its stores, and means the toddler is less demanding when the new baby is born. In modern Western societies where there is no shortage of food and breastfeeding tends to be briefer, pregnancies can be closer together without any serious risks to the mother.

If the gap between births is only about one year, there is an increased risk of the next baby being born prematurely and/or with a low birthweight. If the birth interval is increased to two years, these risks are greatly reduced. However, all women have individual circumstances, and if for one reason or another the interval between births is about 12–18 months, it may be appropriate for a woman to take vitamin and/or mineral supplements, especially if she has breastfed the previous baby. Whether vitamin/mineral supplements are appropriate or not, it is still very important that great attention is given to making sure you follow a healthy diet which provides all the essential nutrients.

Women with more than four children

It is rather a sweeping statement to say that women who already have four children are at special risk of developing problems in subsequent pregnancies. In fact, the risks are only associated with women who have had small intervals (of, say, less than 18 months) between the previous babies, women who are seriously underweight or overweight, or who are anaemic. Again, it may be appropriate for such women to have vitamin/mineral supplements (particularly iron) before conceiving.

Women who are vegetarian or vegan

Vegetarian and vegan diets can be extremely healthy. However, if you choose simply to cut out meat or fish or dairy foods (or all of these) without ensuring that the nutrients that these foods provide are replaced from other food sources, you may become anaemic or underweight, or develop low body stores of calcium. By following the advice given on pages 86–89 and referring to Appendices 1 and 2 you can ensure that your vegetarian/vegen diet is comprehensive. If you want further advice about vegetarianism/veganism during pregnancy, ask your midwife, who may then refer you to a dietitian or contact the vegetarian/vegan societies listed in Appendix 3.

Teenagers

Teenagers, especially if aged sixteen or under, have increased nutrient requirements during pregnancy to cover the growth of a baby and also to finish their own growth and development. Calcium, iron and some vitamins are particularly important and Chapter 4 gives details about how to achieve adequate dietary intakes.

Women with a limited food budget

Several surveys have shown that women tend to 'go without food' themselves in order to ensure that other members of their family get enough to eat. Both children and partners tend to get priority over women's own needs. A survey in 1991 by the National Children's Home found that over half of mothers on state benefits had gone without some food in order to see their children fed. The same study found that nearly half of all mothers (whether on state benefits or not) routinely went without breakfast, barely a third of the sample ate a piece of fresh fruit each day and less then half ate some green vegetables or salad vegetables each day.

A report by the London Food Commission, using data from the most recent UK dietary intake survey, compared the nutrient intakes of women on a wide range of incomes with the Department of Health's recommended intakes. The report showed that many women, especially those on low incomes, were eating diets that did not provide the recommended levels of vitamins and minerals. The diet of over 25 per cent of women on low incomes appeared to fall below 'almost certain deficiency' levels for eight essential nutrients, i.e. iron, potassium, magnesium, calcium, vitamin A, thiamin, riboflavin and pyridoxine.

It is not impossible to eat a healthy diet whilst on a low income but it is difficult and requires a lot of time spent shopping around; pages 174 to 178 in Appendix 2 give more advice about eating on a budget.

Women with existing medical disorders

This section includes advice for women with food allergies, malabsorption syndrome, diabetes mellitus, and eating disorders. All these conditions involve a certain degree of dietary restriction. When planning a pregnancy it is important to ensure that the dietary restrictions do not lead to nutrient deficiencies and that they allow the increased nutrient requirements of pregnancy to be met.

FOOD ALLERGIES

Food allergies should always be medically diagnosed rather than self-diagnosed. Common food allergies include meat, fish, wheat, milk and dairy products. If a food allergy has been properly diagnosed then it is more than likely that a dietitian will have

15

reviewed the diet and advised alternative sources of deficient nutrients. If this is not the case, ask to be referred to your local dietitian before planning a pregnancy.

MALABSORPTION SYNDROME

Malabsorption occurs in diseases such as coeliac disease, cystic fibrosis, Crohn's disease and ulcerative colitis. It involves a failure to absorb one or more nutrients from the gut, because the gut lining is not working efficiently. Again, a dietitian should be consulted to check that appropriate supplements are provided to make up for any nutritional deficiencies.

DIABETES MELLITUS

Women with diabetes mellitus, whether they need to take insulin injections or not, need to plan for pregnancy very carefully. A diabetic woman should always inform the doctor in charge of her diabetic care that she would like to conceive so that diabetic control can be tightened up. There is little doubt that the risk of having a malformed baby can be reduced for diabetic women by improved blood sugar control. (There is also another type of diabetes that develops during pregnancy called gestational diabetes.)

EATING DISORDERS

The main eating disorders that affect women are anorexia nervosa, bulimia nervosa and binge eating. Anorexia nervosa in its extreme form involves a desire by a woman to maintain her body weight at a level much lower than it should be and yet she still feels fat. It can be a life-threatening disease and apart from self-induced food restriction it can also involve excessive physical exercise to burn up energy (calories) and the use of laxatives so that the food eaten is not absorbed. Bulimia nervosa involves periods of eating normal amounts of food followed by food binges then self-induced vomiting and laxative use so that the food is not fully absorbed. The incidence of women with bulimia is now known to be much higher than originally thought, but there are many degrees of the illness. These range from women who are not happy with their size and shape and try to control it by constant dieting and exercise, to women who feel totally unable to control their food intake and body size. Binge eating has not been formally classified as a disorder distinct from bulimia nervosa but it is used to describe individuals who have problems with recurrent binge eating but who do not engage in the compensatory behaviours of vomiting or the use of laxatives and consequently are obese. The prevalence of all these disorders is very difficult to obtain because individuals often do not seek help, but it has been reported that possibly 20 per cent of 15–30-year-old women have symptoms to some degree.

If eating disorders lead to a very low body weight then quite often periods will cease and a woman will be unable to conceive. Women suffering from eating disorders will frequently have a very poor nutritional status because of a combination of self-induced food restriction and non-absorption of nutrients from food. There is also some evidence that women with eating disorders are more likely to suffer from severe forms of pregnancy sickness.

Women with eating disorders should seek help before conceiving. Often it is a matter of trying to improve their sense of self-esteem, which leads to them feeling better about themselves, even if their body shape is not the same as the 'perfect' one displayed in many women's magazines. There are a number of counsellors available to help with eating disorder problems and the address of a support organization is given in Appendix 3.

FOODS AND NUTRIENTS THAT SHOULD BE LIMITED BEFORE CONCEPTION AND DURING EARLY PREGNANCY

Vitamin A

Vitamin A is supplied to the body in two forms: retinol, which is present in animal and fish food sources, and carotene, which is found in plant foods (see Table 5 in Appendix 2 for more information about food sources). Retinol is stored by the body and very high intakes are toxic, whereas high intakes of carotene are not dangerous. A link between the incidence of some birth defects and excessive retinol intakes has been demonstrated. The Department of Health has repeatedly advised that daily intakes of retinol should not exceed 3,300 mcg, which is four times the recommended daily intake of 750 mcg.

Women who may become pregnant should avoid vitamin and fish oil supplements providing more than 750 mcg of retinol per day.

There are two types of fish oil supplements:

1   those made from the fish liver (e.g. cod liver oil and halibut liver oil), which are very high in retinol and should be avoided.
2   those made from the body of the fish (e.g. Pulse by Seven Seas), which do not contain liver oils and have an almost negligible retinol content.

Always check with your midwife, GP or pharmacist that the brand or supplement you have chosen is safe for pregnancy. There is no danger attached to the taking of supplements containing Vitamin A in the form of carotene, or of consuming a diet rich in carotene.

The Department of Health has advised that all women of childbearing age should avoid liver and liver products such as pâté and sausage because of the very high levels of retinol found in recent analysis of commonly consumed animal livers.

Vitamin supplements

A vitamin is defined as a complex chemical needed by the body in a small amount, i.e. a micronutrient, which must be obtained from the diet either because the body cannot make it or because it cannot make enough of it. In order for a chemical to be known as a vitamin, a lack of it must produce a deficiency disease, and a supply will cure that deficiency, for example, Vitamin C, which is also known as ascorbic acid, will cure the deficiency disease scurvy.

In other words vitamins are essential for humans to function, but if a small amount of a vitamin is so beneficial then it seems logical that, if you take large amounts either from food or as supplements, you will be even healthier. However, that is not the case – taking large amounts of vitamins is as harmful as not taking enough.

Traditionally the British public has been advised by health professionals that if they follow the healthy eating guidelines similar to those outlined in Chapters 3 and 4, and eat a wide variety of foods, they are not likely to become deficient or lacking in any vitamins. Organic food producers argue that the food we eat today is lacking in vitamins because they have been lost during intensive farming and food production, and it is only organically grown food (i.e. food grown without the use of pesticides, herbicides and growth-promoting chemicals) that will have a reasonable vitamin content. Vitamin producers and manufacturers promote their products, usually in a fairly innocuous way, by claiming that it is only vulnerable groups such as pregnant and breastfeeding women, children, the elderly or those recovering from illness and surgery, that need vitamin supplements. Some nutrition experts are now advising that certain vitamins such as beta-carotene (a form of Vitamin A) and Vitamins C and E, which are known as the antioxidant or ACE vitamins, are required not only to prevent deficiency diseases but, if taken in larger amounts, give protection from diseases such as heart disease and cancer. (See page 78 for more information on the ACE vitamins.)

With all this conflicting information it is difficult to know whether or not you need or should take vitamin supplements. The research evidence (apart from that for the vitamin folic acid (see page 6) and Vitamin A (see page 17) is inconclusive, but on balance if you are planning a pregnancy and have recently not been eating well, or have been ill, or have lost body weight, or have an inappropriate body weight according to the chart on pages 10–11, then it is prudent to take a supplement of multivitamins. However, always check with your GP, midwife or pharmacist before taking any supplements that they are suitable for pregnancy.

Alternative nutritionists may analyse the hair from you or your partner to try to detect vitamin deficiencies and then promote supplements to remedy them, thereby 'guaranteeing you' a healthy baby. Nobody can guarantee you a healthy baby because nature is unpredictable. All we can do is promote the guidelines for you to follow to maximize your chances. We advise you to be cautious about following the advice of alternative therapists; hair analysis cannot accurately identify vitamin deficiencies and you should not take the supplements suggested unless you first check their suitability for pregnancy.

Herbal teas and remedies

Herbal preparations in the form of teas, infusions, tablets and medicines are widely available. Some are not advisable during pregnancy (see Chapter 5, page 118), so check with your midwife, GP or pharmacist that any you take are safe to continue during pregnancy.

Foods that should be avoided

There are a variety of foods which are high-risk foods for pregnant women because of their possible contamination with the micro-organisms such as salmonella, listeria or toxoplasma. The effects of these infections are often most severe in early pregnancy, so read Chapter 5 for guidelines about these foods and other food safety measures to minimize the risk of infection.

Alcohol

Alcohol is a poison which can cause miscarriage and damage the developing baby when taken to excess (see Chapter 5). When planning a pregnancy many women do give up drinking alcohol and this seems a sensible practice, but there is no evidence of harm to the baby from small amounts of alcohol, i.e. 1 unit per day, which is equivalent to half a pint of ordinary strength bitter or lager, a pub measure of spirits or one glass of wine (see Table 22 in Appendix 2), during the pre-pregnancy period.

DIET-RELATED QUESTIONS OFTEN ASKED BY WOMEN PLANNING A PREGNANCY

Can what I eat affect the sex of my baby?
There are many old wives' tales about how to increase the chances of having a baby of one sex or another. We are not aware of any which have proved successful – but would be pleased to hear from anyone who is convinced!

What about Dad – should he make any changes?
We have not left out the father because his contribution is unimportant. As the sperm brings half of the genetic material which defines what the baby will be like, and indeed determines its sex, the father's role is clearly vital. The problem with commenting on the father in the preconceptual period is that at the moment we know very little. A lot of research has gone into defining what is normal in terms of numbers of sperms and their ability to fertilize, but there is a great deal still to learn. For instance, something which damaged the chromosomes of the egg cell (ovum) in the mother could have a devastating effect on the baby's development. A similar problem in the father might damage some of the individual sperms but leave millions of the rest in a healthy state. We do not know for sure but it seems probable that the normal healthy sperm is more likely to be

successful in the race to fertilize the egg. Fathers who smoke may have more malformed babies than non-smoking fathers. Hard exercise seems to reduce the sperm count and this might be important for men whose sperm count is low to begin with.

Does being on the contraceptive pill affect my nutritional status?
The older types of contraceptive pill, which were of higher doses of hormones than modern pills, were found to cause a small reduction in blood protein levels, as well as reductions in some of the B vitamins, Vitamin C and zinc. There is no evidence that these alterations in blood levels are likely to cause any problems when planning a pregnancy, and indeed they return to normal within two months when the pill is discontinued. Many studies have looked at whether babies born to mothers taking or just after taking the pill are more likely to be malformed or handicapped and there is no evidence of this.

Could my diet be the cause of my recent miscarriage?
For some couples the reason for pre-pregnancy planning is to try to prevent previous problems recurring. Such problems might include miscarriage, stillborn babies or babies which have died in the first days or weeks of life. They might include babies born with malformations or mental handicaps. Other concerns might relate to the previous pregnancy if, for example, it was complicated by excessive vomiting or blood pressure problems. There might be worries that a particularly painful labour or difficult birth could be a problem again. In all of these circumstances it would be right to discuss matters with the midwife, GP or hospital specialist.

Specifically, as regards miscarriages, these are a very common pregnancy occurrence, affecting 10–15 per cent of all pregnancies. Some miscarriages are found to have occurred because the developing baby had malformations, but in most instances it is not possible to find the cause. Dietary factors, such as deficiencies of vitamins or minerals and reduced food intake due to pregnancy nausea and vomiting, have been investigated but no relationship with miscarriage has been found. In a very few cases, a miscarriage may be caused because the developing baby has caught the infection listeriosis, transmitted by the mother, who may have eaten a high-risk food (see Chapter 5). Cigarette smoking and heavy alcohol drinking do, however, increase the risk of miscarriage.

Is it true that women trying to conceive should not drink coffee?
There have been concerns that high caffeine intakes through coffee drinking can be a cause of difficulty in becoming pregnant. Recent research does not support this. Very high caffeine intakes during pregnancy may not be advisable, however (see page 102).

CHAPTER TWO

Baby on the Way

The body of a healthy woman differs from that of a healthy man when you compare the proportion of their bodies made up of fat and water. After puberty the body of a well-nourished woman is about 25 per cent fat and 50 per cent water, whereas the body of a man contains about 15 per cent fat and 60 per cent water. It is now thought likely that the differences between healthy adult men and women are part of the preparation of a woman's body for future childbearing. The extra fat distributed around her body is there as a reserve of energy to help her to nourish the baby when she becomes pregnant and it is probably particularly important if, for any reason, she does not get an adequate diet. Nausea and vomiting occur most commonly in early pregnancy, and it is reassuring to know that there is plenty of energy available in the mother's body to support the baby's growth even when she is feeling too sick to eat.

Major changes take place in the body soon after the hormones (which confirm that there is a pregnancy) start to circulate in her blood. Typically the changes occur very early in pregnancy and before the developing baby has grown to a size at which it will make any serious demands for nutrition from the mother. In most women the changes which take place in the body are far in excess of the baby's needs and therefore there is a wide cushion of safety. The mother's body changes to make conditions for the developing baby as favourable as possible, although some of these conditions can make the mother herself uncomfortable.

A typical change is for her rate and depth of breathing to increase. The effect of this is to encourage an easier disposal of waste products and gases from the baby across the placenta to the mother, but for the mother it can lead to a feeling of breathlessness. Some women find this uncomfortable through most of their pregnancy. The amount of blood which is circulating also increases considerably and this puts a demand on the heart, which copes by pumping more blood every time it beats and also by beating more often. The increased amount of blood is required to feed the placenta and to help the baby with its growth and development.

Another change that occurs is an increase in blood flow to the kidneys. This again is designed to help the baby get rid of its waste products via the placenta and the mother's blood circulation. The effect the mother might notice, however, is an increase in the amount of urine she produces, and a need to pass urine more often. In fact some women diagnose their own pregnancy when they find themselves passing more urine than usual. The kidneys are being asked to work much harder than they do when the mother is not pregnant and the mechanism by which the kidneys save nutrients such as sugar and amino acids (the building blocks of protein) does not function so well. This results in some women losing quite a lot of these nutrients in the urine. This is not really a problem unless the mother has a very poor diet, but one of the interesting effects is to make a positive urine test for sugar quite common. Nearly two-thirds of healthy women have sugar in their urine at some time while they are pregnant. For non-pregnant women and men, sugar in the urine is a serious sign which may mean that they are developing diabetes, but in pregnancy it is very common in healthy women and very rarely means a problem with diabetes.

Other changes which may be obvious to the mother are an increased blood flow to the skin, making the veins on the backs of the hands and arms stand out more. The hands and feet tend to be warm and rather pink because of the extra blood flowing there. Obviously the breasts get bigger in preparation for producing milk after the baby has been born and particularly in a first pregnancy women will notice changes in the nipples, which become larger and darker in colour. Of course inside the body the biggest change which takes place is the growth of the uterus or womb. The non-pregnant womb weighs only about 55 g (2 oz) if the blood is squeezed out of it, but a womb at the end of pregnancy treated in the same way would weigh about 1 kg (2 lb).

EXERCISE IN EARLY PREGNANCY

Many women who are physically fit and active before the onset of pregnancy make a conscious or subconscious decision to reduce their exercise level when they become pregnant. Studies performed in the United States on recreational runners, aerobic dance instructors and aerobic class participants showed than on average these women decreased their exercise performance by about 14 per cent in the first month of pregnancy and by a further 6–10 per cent in the second month of pregnancy. The reasons for this reduction were related to the symptoms of early pregnancy, in particular generalized feelings of excessive fatigue and nausea. Other women found that the common feeling of breathlessness experienced in early pregnancy made them decrease the amount of exercise they took. Having said this there was a lot of variation amongst individuals. Another part of this study, which is continuing in the United States, is to look at the miscarriage rate in these groups of women compared to fit, healthy pregnant women who do not take regular exercise. So far there is no difference between the groups in the miscarriage rate, nor amongst those who exercise is there any difference in the intensity of exercise between those who miscarry and those who do not. Very little is known about birth deformities and the amount of exercise the mother takes, but studies so far do not suggest that exercise in pregnancy either protects against the conception of babies with something wrong with them or makes the situation worse.

EFFECTS OF EXERCISE

During exercise the muscles use up extra oxygen and require glucose and other sources of energy for the extra work. It has been shown that mild to moderate exercise for up to an hour can be performed without a fall in the level of sugar in the blood. In pregnancy there is already an increase in the amount of oxygen the body requires and of course this would be increased further by exercise, but the body copes very well with this and within reason the amounts of oxygen in the blood do not fall. The heart rate in pregnant women is normally about 14 beats a minute higher than in the non-pregnant woman (i.e. around 84 beats per minute rather than 70). In response to exercise the heart beats more frequently, with rises up to 140 beats per minute with moderate exercise and perhaps 170 beats per minute with strenuous exercise.

The next question is how the baby responds when the mother is exercising. Quite a lot of work has been done on this. Most of the investigators have looked at either the heart rate of the unborn baby or the blood flow, using a technique known as Doppler. The concern is that if the mother's oxygen supply is being diverted to her exercising muscles there may not be enough oxygen to go to the womb to supply the baby. Generally speaking the evidence is that the baby responds to the mother's exercise by increasing its heart rate slightly. This would have the effect of passing more oxygen round the baby's body and, by and large, the baby tolerates mild to moderate exercise without any obvious distress. In one interesting study mothers who were known to be fit were even observed taking exercise during labour! The result of this was no change in the baby's heart rate, leading to the conclusion that no harm to the baby resulted from mild to moderate exercise.

The most worrying association with exercise is perhaps when exercise leads to a significant rise in the body temperature, and it would appear that this can be harmful if prolonged. Fortunately during pregnancy women seem to be more efficient at getting rid of the heat generated by exercise and indeed in late pregnancy the normal body temperature is slightly lower than in early pregnancy or before becoming pregnant.

Another concern is the effect of the hormones of pregnancy on the joints and the supporting tissues which hold the joints in a stable position – the ligaments. Perhaps in preparation for labour, the ligaments and supporting tissue of the skeleton in pregnant women are more relaxed. This clearly has an advantage in terms of the increased flexibility of the bones and joints surrounding the birth canal which will allow the baby more room during the birth process. It has the disadvantage, however, that this increase in elasticity of the joints in the lower back can lead to backache. This softening of the ligaments can also be a problem during exercise as overstretching of the joints might lead to injury. This rather limits the type of exercise which is appropriate.

An additional concern is the effect of the weight of the womb on the returning blood flow from the legs. Many pregnant women are aware that they cannot rest comfortably on their back because they get a feeling of faintness. This is simply the result of the pressure of the heavy womb on the large blood vessels which bring the blood back from the legs and lower body towards the heart. The symptom of faintness is easily overcome by the woman moving over on to her side, but this does mean that from about four months of pregnancy exercise which involves lying directly on the back is probably not a good idea.

The energy consumed during exercise in pregnancy is an interesting question on which recent research has been performed. One would imagine that carrying the extra weight of the pregnancy and the increased amount of blood in the mother's body means that to do the same sort of exercise whilst she is pregnant requires expenditure of more energy. It seems that for about half of healthy pregnant women this is true but the other half are very energy-efficient whilst pregnant. They can often do both weight-bearing and non-weight-bearing exercise in the first half of pregnancy with an expenditure of less energy than when they are not pregnant! This means that as far as energy (calorie) intake is concerned the sensible option is again to be guided by appetite rather than feeling under any obligation to eat extra food because of the exercise pattern.

RECOMMENDATIONS ABOUT EXERCISE

Deciding about the most appropriate kind of exercise depends on the course of pregnancy and any complications which develop, and the level of fitness which a woman had before she became pregnant.

There seems no reason why exercise should not be undertaken during a healthy pregnancy. When things go wrong in pregnancy, such as a rise in blood pressure, more rest is needed and the amount of exercise should probably be reduced. The average woman taking a reasonable amount of exercise should expect to continue either her normal activity level or something slightly less whilst pregnant, though athletes in heavy training and women who are unused to any exercise need to approach matters differently. The extremely active woman should reduce her level of activity to non-strenuous levels and in particular should avoid dehydration (her body becoming short of fluid) and prolonged rises in body temperature. Those who are not used to exercise at all should probably not *start* strenuous exercise whilst pregnant, but might think positively about the time after the birth as an opportunity to develop a pattern of regular exercise.

Those types of exercise which can be safely recommended include walking, jogging, cycling and swimming, including aquarobics. Exercise activities which require sudden changes of direction should be avoided, as should anything which might lead to loads directly on the abdomen or sports which involve jumping. It is best to opt out of competitive sports during pregnancy and also to avoid exercise at high altitude or in conditions of heat or high humidity.

The American College of Obstetricians and Gynecologists has offered the following guidelines for exercise during pregnancy and after delivery:

1 Maternal heart rate should not exceed 140 beats per minute.
2 Strenuous activities should not exceed 15 minutes' duration.
3 No exercise in the supine position (directly on the back) after four months of pregnancy.

4 Calorie intake should be sufficient to meet the needs of the pregnancy and the exercise.
5 Mother's temperature should not exceed 38°C.
6 Regular exercise is preferable to intermittent exercise.
7 Vigorous exercise should not be performed in hot or humid weather or if the mother has a temperature for any other reason.
8 Jerky movements should be avoided.
9 Joints should not be taken to the point of maximum resistance during stretching.
10 Liquid should be taken liberally before and after exercise.
11 Exercise should be stopped if any unusual symptoms appear.

PHYSICAL WORK DURING PREGNANCY

The comments about exercise and pregnancy have been written from the point of view of the woman who has a choice whether to exercise or not and of course it is a common pattern, in Western societies at least, for women to rest more and do less exercise and work as the pregnancy advances. In many situations, and particularly in Third World countries, women do not have this luxury and are involved in heavy physical work until quite late in their pregnancy. It should be pointed out before the following remarks that although we summarize below studies which have been done on women in the workplace, no good studies have been done about domestic work and childcare, which represent the major physical activity of many pregnant women.

Work in a standing position

Women who work in a standing position do not seem to have more miscarriages, but there is some evidence (although the studies are conflicting) that babies born to mothers who work in a standing position into late pregnancy are slightly smaller than those born to women whose work is in a sitting position. Some, but not all, reports have noticed a slight increase in the number of babies born prematurely in women who work in a standing position.

Effects of lifting

Occasional lifting does not seem to be a problem, but there does appear to be a slight increase in both miscarriage rates and premature birth in women who do frequent heavy lifting whilst pregnant. There is no evidence that this type of work affects the birthweight of the baby.

Other strenuous jobs

One study from France suggested that the rate of premature births is higher in women with occupational fatigue, but elsewhere the evidence is less convincing and there doesn't seem to be a serious effect on birthweight or miscarriage rates. Some observations which have been made in the Third World do link hard physical work in the second half of the pregnancy with smaller birthweight which could be avoided by taking more rest. Some of the women who were looked at in these reports were suffering from a shortage of food energy as well.

THE GROWTH OF THE BABY

Ovulation, the production of an egg cell by the mother, takes place approximately 14 days after the first day of the last menstrual period. If fertilization occurs it is in the outside part of the uterine tube nearest to the ovaries about 12 to 24 hours after ovulation. The fertilized egg starts to divide into new cells immediately after fertilization and also continues its journey down the uterine tube towards the cavity of the womb. It arrives in the womb about four days after fertilization and after five and a half or six days attaches itself to the wall of the womb, a process known as implantation.

Although it is conventional to talk about the duration of pregnancy from the date of the first missed period you will see that it is actually more accurate to talk about the duration of pregnancy from the time of fertilization, which is two weeks later (see chart on pages 34–35). Soon after implantation has taken place the cells which are going to form the placenta or afterbirth (the trophoblast) start to burrow into the lining of the womb and they also produce a hormone, human chorionic gonadotrophin or hCG, which is the substance which is detected in a pregnancy test. Modern ultrasensitive pregnancy tests may therefore be able to confirm the presence of a developing pregnancy even before the first missed period. The length of time from fertilization up until about the 12th week is called the time of embryogenesis (formation of the embryo) and it is during this critical stage of the pregnancy that all the parts of the baby are formed. At the end of the embryogenesis the baby is tiny but all the important organs can be recognized. After embryogenesis the rest of the pregnancy is called the fetal period of life and during this time the baby increases in size and its organs reach a suitably mature form before birth.

We are particularly interested in the period around the time of fertilization and embryogenesis as it does seem that if things go wrong at this stage the baby can be damaged. A severely damaged baby is normally recognized by the womb in ways we do not yet understand and miscarriage will often take place as a result. This is especially true if the baby has got the wrong number of chromosomes, a condition which would commonly lead to handicap. It is interesting to note when the different parts of the embryo are formed as this can give us some information about when in pregnancy something went wrong if the baby is subsequently found to have developed an abnormality.

As can be seen in the chart overleaf, the central nervous system (brain and spinal cord) is principally developing between weeks

3 to 6 after fertilization (5th to 8th weeks of pregnancy). The heart is also being formed at this time and its development is completed towards the end of the 6th week after fertilization. The ears, eyes and limbs begin to develop during the 4th week after fertilization. The development of the limbs is more or less complete by the 8th week after fertilization, the eyes a few days later and the ears by the middle of the ninth week after fertilization. The lips are formed during weeks 5 and 6 (7th and 8th weeks of pregnancy); the teeth and the palate principally develop during weeks 7 and 8 after fertilization (9th and 10th weeks of pregnancy) and the sexual organs during weeks 7, 8 and 9 after fertilization.

From about 10 weeks after the missed period (i.e. 8 weeks after fertilization) a harmful stimulus will not cause structural abnormalities, but it may affect the growth and function of the various parts of the body. An example here is German measles (rubella), which if caught in the early part of pregnancy during embryogenesis can lead to major handicapping abnormalities of the baby such as a failure of the eyes to form, or defects in the heart and brain which may lead to mental retardation. If caught later in pregnancy the same virus may lead to deafness and some slowing of growth of the baby but not the same severe bodily malformations.

A second example is the drug Thalidomide, which caused severe abnormalities or even the absence of the limbs of babies if the mother took it in the early stages of pregnancy. Looking back at the evidence, the embryo was most vulnerable to this damage if the mother took the drug during the 7th week after the last menstrual period, that is the 5th week after conception. In the case of spina bifida, which is discussed later, damage to the spinal column happens if the mother does not take enough folate in her diet in the very earliest weeks after conception, perhaps even at the time when fertilization has just taken place.

The chart overleaf also shows in illustrative form the development of a normal baby and gives the weight and length of the baby as weeks go by. The table following gives greater detail of the average length and weight of a developing baby.

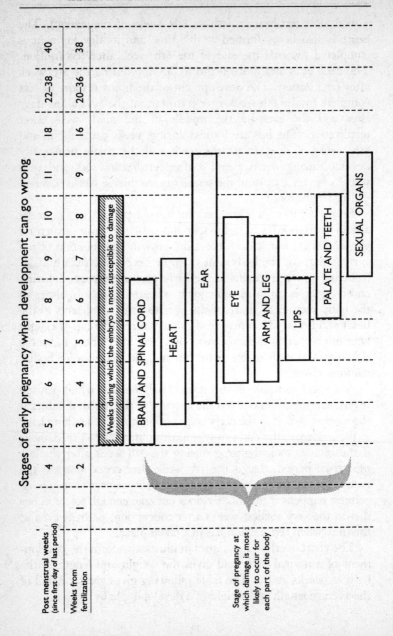

Stages of early pregnancy when development can go wrong

| Post menstrual weeks (since first day of last period) | 1 | | | 4 | 5 | 6 | 7 | 8 | 9 | 10 | 11 | | 18 | 22–38 | | 40 |
| Weeks from fertilization | | | | 2 | 3 | 4 | 5 | 6 | 7 | 8 | 9 | | 16 | 20–36 | | 38 |

Weeks during which the embryo is most susceptible to damage

BRAIN AND SPINAL CORD

HEART

EAR

EYE

ARM AND LEG

LIPS

PALATE AND TEETH

SEXUAL ORGANS

Stage of pregnancy at which damage is most likely to occur for each part of the body

Development of a normal baby

THE EMBRYO

THE FETUS

Weight (grammes)	3	4								10–45	250–450	500–2900	3000–3400
Length (cms)			5	6	7	8	9	10		5–8	15–19	20–34	35–36
Post menstrual weeks (since first day of last period)	1	2	3	4	5	6	7	8	9	10	11	18	22–38	40
Weeks from fertilization										8	9	16	20–36	38

Average length and weight of the developing baby

Weeks since last menstrual period	Length of the baby from top of head to bottom (cm)	Weight (in gm)
9–12	5–8	10–45
13–16	9–14	60–200
17–20	15–19	250–450
21–24	20–23	500–820
25–28	24–27	900–1300
29–32	28–30	1400–2100
33–36	31–34	2200–2900
37–40	35–36	3000–3400

HOW THE PLACENTA WORKS AND HOW NUTRIENTS PASS TO THE BABY

The placenta, or afterbirth, forms the vital link between the developing baby in the womb and its mother. People tend to think of it as something different from the baby, perhaps because it is delivered a few minutes after the baby when the new parents' attention is elsewhere. Some scientists even talk about the fetal-placental unit as if they were two things which come together, but of course it is not like this, the placenta is a part of the developing baby and a very important part from the earliest stages of pregnancy.

When the cells which are developed from the fertilized egg reach the womb they select a part of the wall of the womb on which to attach themselves and new cells which will form the placenta burrow into the mother's tissues like a little parasite. As the embryo develops and gets its own blood circulation the blood is carried to the placenta by the embryo's heartbeat. The circulation of the baby and the circulation of the mother almost come into contact, although they are always separated by two thin layers of cells. As the placenta develops it has a structure which allows the tiny blood vessels of the baby to be surrounded by the flow of the mother's blood to the placenta.

When we think about what the placenta does, we think first

36

about oxygen coming from the mother's blood into the baby's blood as well as nutrition for the baby in the form of carbohydrates, proteins and fats. The placenta obviously has an important function in getting rid of the baby's waste products, such as carbon dioxide, which returns to the mother's blood to be breathed out through her lungs, and substances such as urea, which are passed out through the mother's kidneys in her urine. The placenta also performs an important function in creating a barrier between the mother and the baby which allows her to tolerate the baby as it grows, and prevents her from rejecting it in the way a skin graft or a kidney graft from a donor might be rejected. Another important function of the placenta is to produce hormones or chemical messengers which send signals both to the developing baby and to the mother herself. In fact it is one of these placental hormones (human chorionic gonadotrophin hCG) which is found in the mother's bloodstream almost as soon as the placenta has started to form. Other hormones produced by the placenta include human placental lactogen (hPL), which has some effect on breakdown of fat in the mother during pregnancy, and therefore has a role in determining what nutrients are available to the developing baby. Because the amount of hPL in the mother's blood rises as the placenta grows it is sometimes used as a test to make sure that the baby with its placenta are developing well.

Oestrogen and progesterone, which outside of pregnancy are produced by the ovary, are also produced in large amounts from the placenta. The oestrogen seems to have a role in the enlargement of the muscular wall of the womb and also in stimulating breast tissue to develop in preparation for breast feeding. The function of the high levels of progesterone is less certain, but one important effect seems to be to relax the muscular wall of the womb as it grows to accommodate the baby as pregnancy advances.

Oxygen supply to the developing baby

The mother's blood, which comes to the placenta from the lungs via the heart, is very rich in oxygen. This is carried in the blood by the red blood cells. When it reaches the placenta the oxygen leaves the mother's red cells and crosses into those of the baby where it is used for essential life processes. The waste gas which comes from these processes is called carbon dioxide and this passes out from the baby across the placenta and into the mother's bloodstream. The level of carbon dioxide in the mother in pregnancy is lower than when she is not pregnant and to hold this blood level at the lower point the pregnant woman has to breathe harder than when she is not pregnant. While this accounts for the common feeling of breathlessness, it also means that the waste gas carbon dioxide can leave the baby's circulation very quickly and easily to enter the mother's circulation.

Water and nutrients

Water passes rapidly across the placenta and it is very easy for the developing baby to get the water it needs from the mother's circulation. Glucose, which represents about three-quarters of the energy requirements of the baby, also crosses the placenta very easily. Proteins in the baby are usually made from amino acids, the basic building blocks of protein which pass from the mother's circulation into the baby, but a few proteins, particularly those involved in immunity to disease (antibodies), can cross from the mother to the baby intact. It is thought that these proteins in the baby's blood have an important role in protecting the baby against infection in the first month or two of life. Unfortunately, some of these proteins, which should be protective, can be harmful to the baby. The best known one is the rhesus antibody which, in a rhesus negative mother who carries the antibody, can cross the placenta into the baby and destroy some of the baby's blood cells, making it anaemic when it is born.

Fats usually cross the placenta in the form of their breakdown products free fatty acids, but can be rebuilt into fat for storage or development within the developing baby on its own side of the placenta. As far as vitamins and minerals are concerned the baby is really a very effective 'parasite' and can usually get most of what it needs from the mother's circulation across the placenta. A good example is iron, which the baby needs to make red blood cells. The mother may be iron deficient and very anaemic but her baby will continue to take iron from her body and will usually be born with all the red cells it requires.

Waste products from the developing baby cross the placenta in the other direction, particuarly urea, which comes from the breakdown of protein in the developing baby. Again the high efficiency of the mother's kidneys in pregnancy lowers the level of urea in her blood so that any which forms in her developing baby crosses the placenta rapidly and is easily passed out through her kidneys.

Unwanted placental transfer

Although the placenta is very efficient in selecting what the baby needs and rejecting what it doesn't, occasionally it can be fooled and some things can cross the placenta which are not wanted. This refers in particularly to some types of drugs and it is important when thinking of any kind of drug treatment in pregnancy to consider whether or not the drug can cross the placenta to the baby and, if it can, whether it can pose a threat to the baby's development or growth. Doctors are aware of these dangers, particularly since the Thalidomide tragedy, and will prescribe a drug which crosses the placenta only if it is essential to the mother's health and there is no alternative available or, in much rarer cases, if they are trying to treat something wrong with the baby whilst it is still in the mother's womb. An example of this would be the steroid drugs sometimes given to mothers to help mature the baby's lungs if the baby has to be delivered prematurely for any reason.

BORN TOO LARGE OR BORN TOO SMALL? INFLUENCES ON BIRTHWEIGHT

The average birthweight of a baby born to parents of European origin is about 3.3 kg (7½ lb), but birthweights from 2.5 kg (5½ lb) up to 4 kg (9 lb) in babies born within two weeks either side of the due date are judged to be normal or acceptable. Doctors tend to worry about babies which are small at birth in case their nutrition has been inadequate or they have got something wrong with them. They also worry about babies which are thought to be big at birth, because there may be difficulty for the mother in delivering a large baby and the baby may be damaged.

Born too small

One of the commonest reasons for a baby being born with a low birthweight is if the baby is born prematurely or before the due date. In many cases we do not know why premature labour or premature birth takes place but it is certainly more common in twin pregnancy, where it is thought the womb cannot grow enough to accommodate two large babies and their placentas. It is also more common where there has been any kind of infection in the mother, or indeed in the membranes surrounding the baby, and it is also seen more often where there has been bleeding in pregnancy, particularly bleeding in the second half of pregnancy. There are also studies which show that premature birth is more common in women who smoke, in women of lower social class, and those who are poorly supported and have unfavourable social backgrounds, such as poor housing. In most cases, however, no real cause can be found.

A small number of babies are delivered prematurely because the mother has a sickness which is either threatening her life or the life of her baby. The commonest example of this is pre-eclampsia or blood pressure problems related to pregnancy where early delivery may be undertaken either by induction of labour or by Caesarean section to preserve the mother's health.

As far as the premature baby is concerned the outlook is much better these days than it used to be. A lot of these babies have problems with breathing and require ventilation (life support machines), but these are now available in most major maternity hospitals and given proper care all but the very tiniest of premature babies can expect to survive and develop like normal babies.

The other type of small baby which causes concern is the one which is born within two weeks either side of the due date but is smaller than average. Doctors tend to talk about 'small for dates' babies and usually they mean that if a hundred newborn babies were lined up according to their birthweight, the smallest ten babies would be the ones they were concerned about. Most of these babies have birthweights under 2.5 kg (5½ lb). The question is whether these babies were exposed to problems in the womb which have stopped them reaching their full potential for growth (which might lead to poor growth and possible handicap in childhood). Other doctors think that it is only the smallest five babies out of a hundred which are a cause for concern. In truth about seven out of the ten smallest babies will be healthy babies of small mothers. Probably the most important influence on a baby's size at birth is the adult height of its mother and it is clearly sensible that small women have small birthweight babies to prevent problems in labour if the baby should be too big for the birth canal. Another consideration in multiethnic societies is the influence of race on birthweight. There is no doubt that Asian and Afro-Caribbean mothers in the UK have babies which are 200–300 g (7–10 oz) smaller on average than European mothers, but this is not usually a cause for concern.

If we accept that seven out of the smallest ten babies are healthy, then it means that three out of the ten are smaller than they might otherwise have been. One of these three babies is likely to have been damaged, either because it has developed abnormally or because it has some abnormality of the chromosomes, such as an extra chromosome (as seen in Down's syndrome for instance), or because it has been exposed to some infection in the womb such as German measles (rubella). The other two small babies will be the ones for whom something has gone wrong during the pregnancy and the possibilities include damage to the placenta or afterbirth which prevents it from transmitting adequate oxygen and/or nutrition to the baby. Damage can arise if the placenta has been disrupted by bleeding underneath it in late pregnancy or sometimes, in women with high blood pressure, if blood vessels close up and cut off blood supplies to areas of it. Another important cause of being born too small is mothers smoking. This seems to operate in two ways. The carbon monoxide from the cigarette smoke is a gas which can interfere with the carriage of oxygen by the red cells in the mother's body and this can reduce the oxygen supply to the baby. Also in mothers who smoke the blood vessels tend to be narrower and the actual amount of blood flowing to the placenta may be reduced.

Maternal nutrition and poor growth

It seems obvious that when women are starved or seriously undernourished in pregnancy it must have an effect on the growth of the baby and this is certainly the case. However, it does not seem to be as bad as one might expect. The baby's growth appears to be protected against acute starvation in the first two-thirds of pregnancy and it is only when the mother has been exposed to famine in the last three months of pregnancy that a reduction in the birthweight is seen. This affects all the babies, not just the small ones, but on average they are only about 220 g (8 oz) lighter.

Causes of high birthweight

Many people would consider it unusual to be worried about a baby being too big. It is commonly thought that a large 'bouncing' baby is by definition a healthy baby. This idea comes from the fact that most of the babies who are sick or who have problems after birth are the smaller babies, but there is no doubt that some big babies are also at risk because of their size. As stated above some large babies have considerable difficulty during the birth, either because the head is too large for the birth canal or if the head passes through the birth canal the shoulders may get stuck leading to asphyxiation of the baby. Doctors are aware of this and usually if the baby is thought to be at risk a Caesarean birth will be offered to the mother.

Of the hundred babies discussed above who were lined up according to birthweight, the ten biggest babies tend to be described as 'large for dates'. Of these ten babies, seven will be healthy large babies born of large (tall) mothers but three of them will be larger than they might otherwise have been because they have had an excess of nutrition during their time in the womb. The usual cause of this is diabetes in the mother, but it is almost as common in women who are overweight at the start of pregnancy or who put on a lot of excess weight during the pregnancy. Some of these overweight mothers have a disorder similar to diabetes which causes them to have a high blood sugar level just during the time when they are pregnant. In many clinics tests are done to try to make this diagnosis, and treatment in the form of special diet or even insulin injections can be offered, which will help to keep down the excessive birthweight.

Twins, triplets and other multiple births

About one pregnancy in 80 in the United Kingdom results in a twin birth and triplets occur in one pregnancy in 6,400, if we exclude the mothers who have required specialist infertility treatment. Nowadays, with modern infertility treatment, particularly the use of drugs to make the mother produce an egg on a monthly cycle or techniques such as in vitro fertilization (test tube babies), twins, triplets or even higher order births are much more common than they would be naturally.

It cannot be disputed that multiple pregnancy does put the babies at extra risk. Perhaps the main concerns are of premature birth, which is particularly common with identical twins, and of blood pressure problems in the mother. This is common with twins but even more so with triplets and quads, where the birth often has to be induced because the blood pressure problems are so severe as to be putting the mother's health at risk. Amongst those twin pregnancies where there is not a premature labour doctors are always concerned to monitor the growth of the two babies. This is because it sometimes happens that one baby has a larger placenta than the other or is getting a better blood supply from its part of a common placenta. Scan tests may show that one baby is growing normally whereas the other is very small and in these pregnancies doctors have to make difficult decisions about when best to recommend delivery since they want the small baby to be born alive but do not want to put the big baby at risk of death from a premature birth.

Generally speaking, where the twins have a reasonably equal share of the placenta they are of small to average weight at birth.

As far as the mother is concerned, when she is carrying twins all the changes discussed earlier in the chapter occur but to a greater degree. She has a higher volume of blood circulating in her body and the heart has to work correspondingly harder to pump the blood to the placentas of two babies rather than one. Sickness and nausea are more common, as is breathlessness, and the mother becomes more tired more quickly as her body adapts to the twin pregnancy and she takes the strain of carrying the extra weight around. With regard to nutrition, there are some concerns that anaemia, for instance, particularly anaemia due to deficiency of folate in the blood, is more common in a twin pregnancy. Many doctors recommend additional iron and folic acid supplements, although this may not always be necessary in well-nourished women.

If a deficiency is arising, this is usually easily recognized from routine blood tests in the antenatal clinic.

WHY WEIGHT GAIN IS IMPORTANT AND WHAT INFLUENCES IT

Normal weight gain

Studies performed a number of years ago in the north east of Scotland on healthy women having their first pregnancy showed that the average weight gain was 12.5 kg (27½ lb). Unfortunately people have taken this figure, which is after all an average one, to be 'normal' and therefore the weight gain which every pregnant woman should strive to achieve. They have suggested that women who are gaining less weight should eat more to try to increase their weight gain and that women who are gaining excess weight should eat less.

The first point to make is that the women in the studies ranged from those who actually lost weight whilst pregnant to some women who gained as much as 23 kg (52 lb). This means that it is very difficult to say with confidence to an apparently healthy pregnant woman that she is gaining either too much or too little weight for her stage of pregnancy, but this often occurs in practice.

Again looking at the average woman the rate of weight gain is slightly slower in the first half of pregnancy, 0.36 kg (12 oz) per week, compared to the second half of pregnancy where the rate is around 0.45 kg (1 lb) per week. The original studies suggested that in the last few weeks of pregnancy the rate of weight gain slowed a little. Surveys have shown that there are more premature births and babies dying for all reasons amongst those women who gain less than 0.25 kg (8 oz) per week and those who gain more than 0.7 kg (1½ lb) per week than amongst the women in the middle whose average weight gain is between 0.25 kg (8 oz) and 0.7 kg (1½ lb) per week. This led to the feeling that there was a weight gain which could be prescribed for pregnant women which would be associated with the most healthy outcome for the pregnancy. Unfortunately things are not that simple. For instance, one of the reasons why women who lose their babies

45

make a poor weight gain is that sick babies tend to be small and have a small amount of liquor (fluid) around them. The poor growth of the baby is therefore a part of the explanation of the poor weight gain and because the baby has something seriously wrong with it this would explain why it dies.

On the other hand, those women who gain more than 0.7 kg (1½ lb) per week also tend to lose more babies. A major explanation of this is the influence of pre-eclampsia (pregnancy blood pressure). We know that this condition can be very serious both for mother and babies but we also know that women who develop this condition also store a lot of excess fluid in their own bodies. We therefore have a situation of a woman who is putting on a lot of weight, which might seem like a good thing, but in fact it is a bad thing because all the extra weight is unwanted fluid.

Some midwives and doctors in fact use regular measurements of weight to pinpoint problems, and of course they are looking at women who gain weight too quickly as well as those who gain weight too slowly. This may be a useful check for some women but of course it is very hard to tell the healthy woman with a normal pregnancy from the woman with the abnormal pregnancy just by looking at the weight pattern.

The components of weight gain

We have already seen that an average baby weighs about 3.4 kg (7½ lb) at birth. The average amount of amniotic fluid (the fluid surrounding the baby) is about 0.8 kg (1½ lb) and the average weight of the placenta (afterbirth) is 0.65 kg (1 lb). The rest of the average weight gain is in the mother's body and consists of 1.4 kg (3 lb) in the womb and breasts, plus about 1.4 kg (3 lb) of extra circulating blood and a similar amount of extra fluid in the tissues outside of the blood vessels. There is also, perhaps surprisingly, an average gain of about 3.5 kg (7½ lb) of fat, or stored energy, on the mother's body.

Other influences on weight gain

ORDER OF BIRTH

The studies we have talked about were all performed on women having their first baby and it is known that such women gain about 1 kg (2 lb) more than women having their second, third or later babies. There are two possible explanations for this. One is that, in a first pregnancy, blood pressure problems and the accompanying fluid retention are more common. The second is that a woman having her first pregnancy may have more opportunities for rest with no small children to care for.

ETHNIC ORIGIN

Afro-Caribbean women and Asian women tend to gain slightly less weight during pregnancy than white women, but this difference does not seem to have any influence on the outcome of the pregnancy and is therefore probably not important.

SMOKING, ALCOHOL AND STREET DRUGS

The use of all these substances in pregnancy can be harmful and can slow the growth of the baby. Many women who are abusing substances of this nature also have a relatively poor diet and for both reasons the weight gain can be low.

SOCIOECONOMIC STATUS

There is an assocation between low socioeconomic status and low weight gain in pregnancy but it would be difficult to identify any single cause for the poor weight gain.

TWIN PREGNANCY

It is obvious that someone carrying a twin pregnancy is likely to have a higher weight gain than somebody with just one baby, but again it is difficult to prescribe a normal weight gain for a woman who is pregnant with twins. The average total weight gain has been calculated at 22 kg (48 lb).

CALORIE (ENERGY) CONSUMPTION

Obviously the amount of food eaten during pregnancy can have an influence on weight gain although the relationships are not simple. Women who have bad nausea and vomiting in early pregnancy or who do not eat very much food in later pregnancy for whatever reason will make a poor weight gain or may even lose weight. The opposite is true of women who overeat whilst they are pregnant who may find that they are depositing a large amount of fat on their bodies which will remain after the baby has been born. The difficulty of relating the amount of food eaten to the weight gain is that each woman appears to be an individual in terms of how rapidly she consumes energy whilst she is pregnant. Some women are very efficient in the use of energy while they are pregnant and tend to store extra energy as fat. Other women are less energy efficient and burn the calories away. At the moment we do not have an easy way of recognizing which type of pattern the individual woman fits into. It is therefore difficult to give advice other than to say that appetite should be your guide.

Weight gain recommendations

Although we have said it is very difficult to advise the individual woman about what her weight gain should be, as pregnancy goes on there are some general guidelines which you may find helpful. These come from the American Institute of Medicine and the advice is based on the body weight before the pregnancy. To find out whether you were underweight, normal or overweight for your height before pregnancy, check the charts on pages 10 and 11. Women who were in band 1, i.e. underweight, before they became pregnant should be encouraged to eat rather more in the hope that their babies will grow better, whereas women who were overweight (bands 3, 4 and 5) at the start of pregnancy have plenty of stored energy for the baby's growth and should avoid eating too much as they may end up becoming even more overweight. The recommendations are as below.

Recommended Total Weight Gain Ranges for Pregnancy based on Pre-pregnancy Weight for Height

Weight for height category	Recommended Total Gain	
	kg	lb
underweight (band 1)	12.5–18	28–40
normal weight (band 2)	11.5–16	25–35
overweight (bands 3, 4 and 5)	7–11.5	15–25

In addition to this, the Institute recommends that teenagers and Afro-Caribbean women should aim for gains at the upper end of the range in the hope of reducing the likelihood of a low birthweight baby.

Short women of less than 157 cm (5 ft 2 in) should aim for gains at the low end of the range as this may prevent them having an excessively large baby which could cause complications during labour and delivery.

Finally, the recommendation to those who are seriously over-weight, i.e. in band 5, is that they should aim for a weight gain of about 6 kg (14 lb). Although it might seem that such women would benefit from calorie restriction whilst they are pregnant, in order to lose some of their fat, a lot of concern has been expressed about the possible effect of reducing the baby's growth. In addition, there is some evidence, from studies done in the United States, that women who are slimming whilst pregnant and thus breaking down their body stores of fat, may have babies with slightly reduced intelligence compared to those women who eat normally whilst pregnant. Further studies are needed in this important area before firm conclusions can be drawn but it is certainly the case that the overweight pregnant woman should only eat to appetite and not take any extra food 'for the baby's sake'.

In conclusion we would advise that those planning a pregnancy correct a deficient diet before actually becoming pregnant and develop good eating patterns which they can continue whilst pregnant. During pregnancy it is reasonable advice to eat to appetite. Although a weight gain in the prescribed ranges may be reassuring, if you find you are making an excessive or a rather smaller than average weight gain it would be worth discussing this with your midwife or doctor, but this certainly does not mean that something is bound to be wrong with the pregnancy.

CHAPTER THREE

The Nutrients that You and Your Baby Need

This chapter describes the recommended amount of individual nutrients for a normal healthy woman and explains how the requirement for some of these increases during pregnancy and whilst breastfeeding. If you find this too detailed go straight to Chapter 4. The tables in Appendix 2 showing dietary sources of these nutrients will help you assess whether your own diet is satisfactory or whether you need to make some changes.

A NOTE ON RECOMMENDED INTAKES OF NUTRIENTS

The British Government Department of Health publishes guidelines about recommended intakes of nutrients or Dietary Reference Values (DRVs) for different groups of the population which are updated every ten years or so. These DRVs are designed to be targets or standards to help ensure that individuals are having the correct amount of calories (energy) and enough of each nutrient to prevent deficiency.

Some of the names for DRVs can be confusing. For example, the requirement for energy is referred to as the Estimated Average Requirement (or EAR), and whilst some women will need more than the figure quoted others may need less, depending mainly on levels of physical activity. The requirements for most other nutrients are expressed as the Reference Nutrient Intake (or RNI) which, if met by your diet, means that you are unlikely to become deficient in that nutrient. Try not to be put off by these terms and abbreviations, just look carefully at the tables in Appendix 2 describing the sources of the individual nutrients and work out if you are getting enough of them. If the answer is no, it should be clear how you may need to change your diet to achieve the nutrient targets.

CALORIE (ENERGY) REQUIREMENTS

Calories are provided by carbohydrate, protein, fat and alcohol (but not by vitamins and minerals). Your body usually uses carbohydrate as its basic fuel or energy source, along with fat, and reserves protein mainly for its tissue-building role. Energy requirements are based on your total intake of carbohydrates, fat and protein and an assumption is made that very few of your calories come from alcohol. Alcohol is not a useful source of calories because it is low in other nutrients.

Calorie (energy) requirements for non-pregnant women

Non-pregnant women aged nineteen to forty-nine years need about 1,940 calories per day; for women aged fifteen to eighteen years the requirement is slightly higher at 2,110 calories. These figures are based on the general population of the UK and assume typical levels of physical activity. For those who are very physically active the calorie requirement is likely to be higher than this. As mentioned previously, these are average figures; some women will need more than this amount and some less. Your body weight is the best guide to your calorie needs. If your weight is stable, and in the normal weight range for your height (see pages 10 and 11), you are having the right amount – if you are losing weight you are not having enough, if you are gaining weight you are having too many. You may find it useful to refer to Table 1 in Appendix 2, which shows the calorie content of a selection of foods.

Calorie (energy) requirements during pregnancy

It may seem logical to you that you need a lot of extra calories during pregnancy for the growth of your baby and to store fat for use during breastfeeding. In fact you actually only need a small extra amount. The reason for this is that your body becomes energy efficient during pregnancy by reducing its metabolic rate, which directly affects your calorie requirement. Reducing your physical activity, which often accompanies pregnancy, further reduces your calorie needs (see Chapter 2 for more information).

These changes mean that for the average woman, no extra calories are required during the first six months of pregnancy and only about 200 extra calories per day are required during the last three months. Two hundred calories is equivalent to two slices of wholemeal toast with margarine or butter, a jacket potato with a small amount of cheese or a large banana with a glass of fresh fruit juice. Women who are underweight at the beginning of pregnancy may need more calories during the whole of their pregnancy.

Appetite is usually the best indication of how much food the individual needs to eat. It may fluctuate during the course of pregnancy. In the first few weeks appetite may reduce dramatically, especially for those suffering from nausea or sickness; at other times you may feel much more hungry than usual. These fluctuations are usually entirely normal, and will not harm the baby.

Calorie (energy) requirements for breastfeeding

Some of the calories required for breast milk production are supplied by body fat reserves which were laid down during pregnancy. However, additional calories are needed over and above your pre-pregnancy intake to ensure enough energy to supply the needs of the growing baby. As weaning proceeds, your calorie needs will gradually return to pre-pregnancy levels. The

UK Department of Health guidelines give two sets of figures for the additional calorie intake required whilst breastfeeding, as shown in the table below. Group 1 mothers are those whose breast milk no longer supplies all or most of the baby's food after the first three months. Group 2 mothers are those who supply all or nearly all the baby's energy and nutrient needs for six months or more.

Additional caloric intake during breastfeeding

Stage of Breastfeeding	Additional EAR (kcal/day)	
Up to 1 month	450	
1 to 2 months	530	
2 to 3 months	570	
	Group 1	Group 2
3 to 6 months	480	570
more than 6 months	240	550

More recent research has suggested that these figures are higher than is observed in practice and that an extra 300–400 calories per day is enough for fully breastfeeding mothers during the first three months.

THE CALORIE-PROVIDING NUTRIENTS

Carbohydrates

Carbohydrate is the basic fuel source for the body. It is metabolized (i.e. chemically processed) to supply calories or energy and 1 gram of carbohydrate will provide approximately 4 calories to the body. It is supplied to your body in two main forms: starch, for example in cereals, bread, rice, pasta, potatoes and yams, and sugar, for example in milk, fruit, 'table sugar' and corn syrup. Sugar can be further divided into sugars that occur naturally in foods, for example in fruits and milk, and processed or refined sugar, i.e. 'table sugar' and added sugar in processed foods and drinks. The Department of Health recommends that carbohydrates supply about half of the calories in your diet and that the majority of these are in the form of starch and sugars which are naturally incorporated in foods. It is advised that no more than 10 per cent of calorie intake (i.e. about 200 calories) is supplied by refined and processed sugars. In a recent survey of UK adults it was found that on average 44 per cent of our calorie intake was supplied by carbohydrates, and that 18 per cent of total calorie intake (about 360 calories) was supplied by refined and processed sugars. Many people therefore need to increase their intake of starchy carbohydrate foods and fruits and vegetables and to decrease their intake of sugary snacks and drinks. The dietary plans in the next chapter will advise you how to make these changes.

DIETARY FIBRE

Dietary fibre is provided from carbohydrate sources and is essential for your body to function properly. Dietary fibre provides bulk to your stools which helps you pass them easily (this is particularly important during pregnancy as constipation is a common problem). Certain forms of fibre also lower blood cholesterol levels (see page 83 for more advice about dietary fibre). Whole grains, legumes, vegetables and fruits are excellent sources of dietary fibre. Table 2 in Appendix 2 lists some of these with the amount of dietary fibre per serving. The UK Department of Health recommends that adult diets should contain on average 18 g per day (individual needs range from 12–24 g per day). Very high dietary fibre intakes, i.e. above 32 g per day, can inhibit absorption of some minerals and are not recommended.

Fats

Fats are also a fuel source, in fact a much more concentrated fuel source than carbohydrates in that they supply over twice the calories per gram as the same weight of carbohydrates, i.e. 1 gram fat provides approximately 9 calories, and they are thus an important fuel for body energy reserves.

There are three main types of fat – saturates, mono-unsaturates and polyunsaturates, and these differ in their structure and also their functions within the body. Saturates make up a large proportion of the fat contained in dairy products, meats and meat products such as sausages and pies, as well as savoury snacks, cakes, biscuits and chocolate. Some vegetable oils (coconut oil and palm oil) are also rich in saturated fat. Saturated fat is not an essential nutrient, and a high fat intake which includes a high proportion of saturated fat increases the risk of coronary heart disease.

People in the UK generally eat too much fat, particularly saturated fat (see pages 86 and 87 for advice on how to reduce your intake and refer to Table 3 in Appendix 2 which gives the fat content of a selection of foods). The Government recommends a reduction of total fat intake to 35 per cent of total calorie intake, and of saturated fat intake to 10 per cent of total calorie intake, from the 40 and 15 per cent respectively that were found in the recent UK national dietary survey.

Foods rich in mono-unsaturates include olive oil (and obviously olives), avocado pears and rapeseed oil, and it is thought that the Mediterranean diet, which features a high intake of mono-unsaturates (along with a high intake of fruit and vegetables) is protective against coronary heart disease.

Polyunsaturates are essential in the diet as they cannot be made in the body. The two essential polyunsaturated fatty acids are linoleic acid, of which the main sources are plant oils, such as sunflower, soya, safflower and corn (maize), and linolenic acid, of which the main sources are oily fish such as sardines, mackerel, salmon and herrings. Essential fatty acids are also thought to contribute to the prevention of heart disease. In addition, it has recently been reported that women from the Faeroe Isles, where the diet is rich in oily fish, have slightly longer pregnancies and their infants slightly higher birth weights in comparison with women whose diets contain very little oily fish. Research studies are now going on to see if this type of diet also reduces the risks of blood pressure complications in pregnancy.

A word of caution, however, about your intake of polyunsaturates. The processing of polyunsaturated fats to make products such as margarine, manufactured cakes and biscuits leads to the production of 'trans-fatty acids', and recently a link between high intakes of these and coronary heart disease has been found. Try to ensure that your intake of polyunsaturates from these sources is not excessive. Continual use of re-heated vegetable oils increases their trans-fatty acid content and it is advisable not to re-heat oils more than once or twice.

Proteins

The functions of dietary protein include

i) repairing and renewing body cells
ii) transporting oxygen and nutrients in the bloodstream
iii) making antibodies to help fight infection
iv) growing and developing the new tissues

Proteins are made up of 'building units' called amino acids into which they are broken down during the digestive process. These amino acids are then used to form the specific protein which your body requires. Some of the amino acids of proteins are 'essential' in that they cannot be manufactured internally by the body and a regular dietary intake is needed. A food protein which supplies all the nine essential amino acids in adequate amounts for humans is called a 'complete' protein. Only animal protein foods such as milk, cheese, eggs and meat are complete proteins. Vegetarians, however, can choose a combination of plant protein foods which together will provide all the essential amino acids (see page 89 and Appendix 1 on pages 168 to 174).

The requirement (RNI) for protein for women aged nineteen to forty-nine years is 45 g per day. (This is based on animal protein intake; a person consuming only vegetable protein may need slightly more.) The extra amount you need during pregnancy is quite small, approximately 6 g per day, and during breastfeeding the additional requirement for protein is at present set at 11 g per day for the first four months and 8 g per day after this. See Table 4 in Appendix 2 to find out the amount of protein in some of the foods you eat.

This intake is almost certainly achieved by almost all UK women at present. The recent UK national dietary survey found that the average protein intake amongst women was 64 g per day. There is some evidence that excessive intakes of protein may be associated with health risks and the Department of Health concluded that it is advisable for adults to avoid protein intakes of more than twice the RNI (i.e. more than 90 g per day for non-pregnant women).

THE NON-CALORIE-SUPPLYING NUTRIENTS

There are two main groups of nutrients – vitamins and minerals – which do not also supply calories. They are vital for life but are needed only in small amounts and are often called micronutrients (from micro meaning small) as opposed to protein, carbohydrate and fats, which are called macronutrients.

VITAMINS

Vitamins are compounds with complex structures whose main role is to increase the speed of chemical reactions within the body. There are two groups of vitamins: the fat-soluble vitamins (A, D, E and K), which can be stored by the body, and the water-soluble (the B-complex vitamins and Vitamin C), which need to be eaten regularly because the body cannot store them.

Fat-soluble vitamins

The table overleaf lists the symptoms associated with deficiencies of the individual fat-soluable vitamins. Deficiencies to this degree are rare in the UK.

Effect of fat-soluble vitamin deficiency in adults

Vitamin	Alternative name	Effect of deficiency
A	Retinol Carotene	Poor vision, dry skin
D	Cholecalciferol	Faulty bone growth
E	Tocopherol	Breakdown of red blood cells & nerve fibres
K	Phylloquinone	Excessive bleeding

VITAMIN A

Vitamin A is supplied to the body in two forms: retinol and beta-carotene. Retinol is provided from animal food sources, whereas beta-carotene is provided from plant food sources. Beta-carotene is then converted by the body to retinol. Vitamin A is needed for the adaptation of the eye to light and dark and also for tissue growth, especially for the skin and mucous membranes (which are your body's first barrier to infection). The RNI (Reference Nutrient Intake) for Vitamin A for women aged fifteen and over is 600 mcg retinol equivalents per day (6 mcg beta-carotene = 1 mcg retinol). During pregnancy this increases to 700 mcg retinol equivalents per day, and during lactation to 950 mcg retinol equivalents per day. Good sources of retinol are offal (but don't forget pregnant women should not eat liver, see page 103), egg yolk, butter or fortified margarine and milk. Good sources of beta-carotene are carrots and green vegetables (especially broccoli, spinach and spring greens). Table 5 in Appendix 2 lists the amount of retinol or beta-carotene in foods so you can check that you are having the correct amount.

The recent dietary survey carried out on a sample of the UK population found the average daily intake of Vitamin A per day amongst women aged twenty-five to thirty-four to be over 1,200 mcg per day, but this average disguised a huge range of intakes, including some women with extremely low intakes, so do check that yours is adequate. On the other hand retinol (Vitamin A from animal sources) is known to be toxic (poisonous) in large amounts (more than 7,500 mcg per day), causing liver and bone damage, hair loss, double vision, vomiting, headaches and other abnormalities. In addition, a link between the incidence of certain birth defects and high retinol intakes during early pregnancy (more than 3,300 mcg per day or four times the RNI) has been suggested and you should therefore avoid eating liver and liver products and taking Vitamin A supplements or fish liver oil supplements at more than the RNI level, both when you are planning a pregnancy and during the first three months. Beta-carotene is not toxic, although very high intakes may lead to a yellow discoloration of the skin.

VITAMIN D

Vitamin D is either produced in the body by the action of sunlight on the skin or is absorbed from food. Its functions include promoting calcium and phosphate absorption and regulating bone calcium metabolism. Many people in the world obtain little or no Vitamin D from their diet, acquiring most from the action of sunlight. In the UK, being outside in the sunshine for short periods between the hours of 11.00 a.m. and 3.00 p.m. during the summer should provide you with enough stores of Vitamin D to last through the winter months. Important dietary sources for those women not regularly exposed to sunlight are oily fish, eggs, fortified margarine and milk. Listed in Table 6 in Appendix 2 are important sources of dietary Vitamin D, and the nutrient content per serving.

There is no RNI for Vitamin D set for non-pregnant women in the UK, the assumption being that a dietary supply is not necessary for individuals living a normal life-style. For those confined indoors the RNI is 10 mcg/day.

The RNI for pregnant women is set at 10 mcg/day and dietary supplementation is recommended to this level. This is a precautionary measure in the event that women are not producing enough Vitamin D from the action of sunlight. Particularly at risk of Vitamin D deficiency are Asian women and women living in the north of England and Scotland who may not be exposed to enough sunlight. The average dietary intake of Vitamin D found amongst women in the recent national dietary survey was 2.6 mcg/day.

VITAMIN E

Vitamin E behaves as an 'antioxidant' in many tissues of the body, which means that it acts to prevent tissue breakdown, particularly protecting cell membranes from damage (see page 79 for more information on the 'antioxidant' vitamins). Vitamin E requirements depend on intakes of polyunsaturated fat, which vary widely, and therefore no recommended intakes have been set. (The higher the polyunsaturated fat intake, the higher the Vitamin E requirement will be.) However, there should be no need for concern, even if intakes of polyunsaturated fats are high, since plant oils high in polyunsaturated fatty acids, for example, are also often high in Vitamin E, so things usually balance out. There are no reports of Vitamin E deficiency amongst adults apart from those people who cannot absorb fat properly. The best food sources are plant oils (such as wheat germ oil, corn oil, sunflower oil and soya oil), nuts and seeds, some fruits and vegetables (such as mango, apple, peaches, sweet potato, avocado, tomato and asparagus) and margarine. Eggs, wholemeal cereals and green leafy vegetables, for example broccoli, are moderately good sources.

Some scientists have recently recommended the taking of supplements of the antioxidant vitamins, including Vitamin E, to offer protection against conditions such as heart disease and cancer. The evidence to support this has not persuaded the majority of research workers and caution is urged due to the possibility of as yet unknown risks attached to high intakes of supplements. This is especially so during pregnancy.

VITAMIN K

Vitamin K is required for the formation of four proteins in the liver which are involved in the blood-clotting process. There have been very few studies of Vitamin K requirements, but most estimates suggest that around 1 mcg per kilogram body weight per day is both safe and adequate. Green leafy vegetables are by far the richest source, but other vegetables, fruits, dairy produce, vegetable oils, cereals and meat can also provide significant amounts.

Water-soluble vitamins

Deficiency symptoms of the water-soluble vitamins are shown in the table opposite. Deficiencies to this extent are extremely rare in the UK.

THIAMIN

Thiamin (Vitamin B1) is required for the body to convert carbohydrate to energy. The more carbohydrate you eat the more thiamin you need. The RNI is based on energy intakes and for all adults this is 0.4 mcg per 1,000 kcal. For a woman consuming the EAR for energy, this translates into about 0.8 mg per day. So extra thiamin is required during pregnancy and lactation only when you take extra calories; the extra 200 calories needed during the last three months of pregnancy would increase thiamin requirements by about 0.05 mcg/day and an extra 500 calories per day during lactation would increase requirements by about 0.2 mcg/day. All animal and plant tissues contain thiamin and it is therefore present in all natural whole foods. Pork, the germ of cereals, nuts, pulses, meat extract (Bovril) and yeast extract (Marmite) are the richest sources. Some vegetables and fruits, eggs and milk contain significant amounts and white bread and breakfast cereals are usually enriched with thiamin. Listed in Table 7 in Appendix 2 are good sources of thiamin with their content per serving.

Effect of water-soluble vitamin deficiency in adults

Vitamin	Alternative name	Effect of dietary deficiency
B1	Thiamin	Appetite loss, nervous tingling, tiredness, fluid retention
B2	Riboflavin	Sore mouth, tongue & eyes, cracks at corner of mouth
Nicotinic acid	Niacin	Appetite loss, tiredness, diarrhoea, itchy flaky skin, confusion
B6	Pyridoxine	Headache, nausea, vomiting, anaemia, flaky skin, sore tongue, depression
Co-enzyme A	Pantothenic acid	Tiredness, headache, nausea
Biotin		Sore tongue, itchy flaky skin, depression
Folic acid	Folate	Anaemia, sore tongue, diarrhoea
B12	Cobalamin	Anaemia
C	Ascorbic acid	Sore gums, poor wound healing

As thiamin is soluble in water, considerable amounts may be lost when cooking vegetables. (See page 84 about reducing the losses of vitamins during cooking.)

RIBOFLAVIN

Riboflavin (Vitamin B2) is necessary for many chemical processes within the body and helps use energy from food efficiently. The RNI for riboflavin for females over eleven years is 1.1 mg per day. The extra need for riboflavin in pregnancy has been estimated as 0.3 mg per day and during lactation 0.5 mg per day. The best sources of this vitamin are dairy products, meats, kidney, eggs, mushrooms, green vegetables, yeast extract (Marmite), meat extract (Bovril) and enriched bread and breakfast cereals. Table 8 in Appendix 2 lists good sources of riboflavin and their content per serving. Considerable losses of riboflavin can also occur when cooking vegetables.

NIACIN

(Vitamin B3) is particularly important in energy production, and its requirement is related to your energy intake. Niacin can actually be made within the body. The RNI for niacin for all women is 6.6 mg niacin per 1,000 calories. For a woman consuming the EAR for energy this translates to about 13.2 mg per day.

During late pregnancy the body becomes more efficient at producing its own niacin and no extra intake is required. However, an increased intake during breastfeeding is advocated to provide for the niacin content of breast milk. This extra demand has been set at 2.3 mg per day. Rich sources of niacin are fish, especially tuna and salmon, meat, mushrooms, wheat bran, yeast extract (Marmite) and peanuts. Enriched bread and breakfast cereals can also provide an important part of the daily niacin requirement. See also Table 9 in Appendix 2. It is estimated that about half the niacin we use is produced within the body. Animal proteins are especially rich in the amino acid tryptophan, which is what the body uses to make its own niacin.

VITAMIN B6

Pyridoxine (Vitamin B6) is necessary for the body to make new protein tissues. Deficiency can result in a form of anaemia (i.e. the oxygen-carrying capacity of the blood is reduced), and in nervous disorders such as depression, headaches and confusion. Very high intakes of Vitamin B6 (in excess of 2 g per day over a period of months) can be dangerous because they can cause nerve damage. This has occurred in women who have taken doses as a way of trying to alleviate the symptoms of premenstrual syndrome.

The RNI for pyridoxine is dependent on your protein intake. For all children over one year and adults the RNI is 15 mcg per gram of protein. For a woman consuming an average protein intake of 64 g, this translates into 15 × 64 mcg per day of pyridoxine, i.e. 960 mcg per day.

Table 10 in Appendix 2 lists rich sources of Vitamin B6. Bananas, watermelon, broccoli and spinach are some of the most nutrient-dense sources. Red meat, fish and poultry are also good sources. Some of the body's pyridoxine comes from natural activity of the bacteria within the gut.

PANTOTHENIC ACID

Pantothenic Acid. This is another B vitamin which is required for energy production. Its name derives from the Greek word 'pantothen', meaning 'from every side', reflecting its widespread supply in foods. Mushrooms, broccoli, eggs, peanuts, meat, milk and many other vegetables are good sources. There has been no RNI set for this vitamin due to the lack of scientific evidence about dietary requirements, but there have been no reported cases of pantothenic acid deficiency in the UK.

BIOTIN

Biotin is required for the body to use the fat in the diet. It is widely distributed in many foods, some of the richer sources being cauliflower, egg yolk, peanuts and cheese. Biotin, like pyridoxine, can be created by bacteria in the healthy gut. Again, no RNI has been set for biotin, and deficiency has never been seen.

FOLIC ACID

Folate/folic acid enters the body either in the form of supplements or by conversion within the body of what we know as folates in food. Folic acid is essential for the creation of new body proteins, and if the body is deficient in it anaemia can develop. This is an easily recognized type of anaemia in which there is a shortage of red blood cells and those which are produced are larger than average.

The RNI for folate for adult women was set at 200 mcg per day, with an increase during pregnancy of 100 mcg per day by the Department of Health in 1991. However, recent research has found that the incidence of neural tube defects such as spina bifida can be reduced if women increase their folate intake above these levels before conception and during the first three months of pregnancy (see page 6). It is now recommended that in this period folic acid supplements are taken (400 mcg per day) and dietary intake is increased to 300 mcg per day. The RNI for folate whilst breastfeeding is 260 mcg per day.

Rich food sources of folate include yeast extract (Marmite), meat extract (Bovril), black-eye beans, leafy green vegetables and orange juice. Unfortunately, inappropriate food preparation and cooking can reduce the folate content of foods; page 84 gives advice on this. Some breads and breakfast cereals are fortified with folic acid, so check the labelling. Table 11 in Appendix 2 lists the good sources of this vitamin.

VITAMIN B12

Cobalamin (Vitamin B12), like folic acid, is important for the formation of red blood cells. In fact the metabolism of cobalamin and folic acid are closely intertwined and thus a deficiency of cobalamin results in the same type of anaemia as folic acid deficiency. Because cobalamin is also involved in nerve cell formation, prolonged deficiency can lead to damage of the nerves of the spinal cord.

The RNI for Vitamin B12 is 1.5 mcg per day with no increase set for pregnancy, on the assumption that body stores contain an adequate amount at the beginning of pregnancy (Vitamin b12 is the exception amongst the water-soluble vitamins in that it can be stored in the body). An increase of 0.5 mcg per day during breastfeeding is advised to ensure an adequate supply in the breast milk. Food sources of cobalamin include almost all animal products; red meats, milk and eggs are the richest sources. Certain algae (for example seaweeds) can synthesize the vitamin, but plant food sources do not usually contain cobalamin. For this reason those following a vegan diet require food supplemented with Vitamin B12, such as fortified soya products (e.g. soya milk), fortified yeast extract (e.g. Marmite) and fortified breakfast cereals. Vegan women should take particular care to ensure an adequate intake of cobalamin during pregnancy, to avoid anaemia. Table 12 in Appendix 2 lists good sources of B12 and the nutrient content per serving.

VITAMIN C

Ascorbic Acid (Vitamin C) is essential for healthy gums, teeth, bones and blood vessels. It is also important for wound healing, resistance to infection, hormone synthesis and iron absorption. It is also an antioxidant (see page 79).

The RNI for Vitamin C for all adults is 40 mg per day. There are claims that higher intakes than this can improve general health, but further research is needed to substantiate this. During pregnancy, especially towards the final stages, there is an extra requirement as the baby takes up the vitamin from the mother's stores. The RNI for the last third of pregnancy is therefore higher, and has been set at 50 mg per day. During breastfeeding the RNI is further increased to 70 mg per day.

Most fruits and vegetables are good sources of Vitamin C, some of the richest being green peppers, cauliflower, broccoli, cabbage, strawberries, citrus fruits and potatoes, as shown in Table 13 in Appendix 2. Smoking dramatically increases the body's requirement for Vitamin C. Intakes of 80 mg per day are required to maintain the same body levels as non-smokers.

Vitamin C is easily destroyed by overcooking vegetables.

Minerals

Minerals, like vitamins, are micronutrients which do not supply energy, but are vital for many of the body's activities within cells. Iron, for instance, prevents anaemia, and calcium is needed both for bones and within muscle cells when they contract. It is not known whether some minerals found in the body, for example vanadium and tin, are necessary to sustain life, although we are aware that others, such as lead and cadmium, have no useful function and can be poisonous (see page 114). The minerals discussed below are those known to be required by the body to maintain health. The symptoms of deficiency are listed in the following table.

Effect of mineral deficiency in adults

Mineral	Effect of dietary deficiency
Calcium	Low intakes may cause osteoporosis in later life.
Phosphorus	Probably none in adults.
Sodium	Muscle cramps.
Potassium	Irregular heart beat, loss of appetite, muscle cramps.
Chloride	Probably none in adults.
Magnesium	Weakness, muscle pain, poor heart function.

CALCIUM

About 99 per cent of the calcium in the body is found in bones and teeth and a plentiful supply of dietary calcium is necessary to maintain adequate levels in them. Calcium is also essential for blood clotting, muscle contraction and nerve signalling. Recent research suggests that having a diet rich in calcium may help to prevent high blood pressure in pregnancy. This is one of the major causes of pre-eclampsia, a condition which can develop in the latter stages of pregnancy (see pages 133–138).

The RNI for calcium for women over eighteen years is 700 mg per day. For fifteen- to eighteen-year-olds it is 800 mg per day. In a recent large UK dietary survey about half the women under thirty-five were not consuming the RNI, so do check that your own calcium intake is adequate. Low calcium intakes are particularly common amongst teenagers.

During pregnancy the body's efficiency at taking calcium from the diet is improved and therefore no increase in calcium intake has been recommended. Additional calcium is required during breastfeeding however, and at present an increase of 550 mg per day is advised. Most breastfeeding women increase their food intake, and therefore their calcium intake usually increases in adequate amounts to supply their milk, but do check Table 14 in Appendix 2 to make sure you are having enough.

Dairy products are the richest sources of calcium. (However, note that most of the calcium in cottage cheese and fromage frais is lost during its production.) Soybean curd (tofu) is also a good source if it is made with calcium carbonate. Many soya milks are also now fortified with calcium (check the labels). White flour has calcium added to it, so anything made from white flour, such as white bread, crackers, pizza bases and pies will be a good source. Leafy green vegetables, especially spinach, contain calcium, but the body is less efficient at absorbing it from these particular foods.

There is no evidence that high intakes of calcium are harmful. Calcium supplementation may be necessary for those avoiding or unable to consume dairy products. However, increasing your dietary supply with other calcium-containing foods is preferable.

PHOSPHORUS

Most of the phosphorus in the body is found in the bones. The rest circulates in the bloodstream or is present inside cells, where it is vital for energy production. The RNIs for phosphorus are the same as for calcium (as these minerals are present in the body in equal amounts) i.e. 700 mg per day for women over eighteen, 800 mg per day for fifteen- to eighteen-year-olds, no increase in pregnancy due to maternal adaptations and an increase of 550 mg per day during breastfeeding.

Phosphorus is found in useful amounts in many foods as it is a major constituent of all plant and animal cells. It is also present in many food additives. Deficiency is therefore very unlikely, especially because it is very well absorbed.

SODIUM

The major role of sodium (often referred to as salt) is the part it plays in maintaining the correct amount of water in the fluid surrounding cells.

The RNI for sodium for anyone over ten years is 1,600 mg per day, with no increase during pregnancy or breastfeeding. Most people in the UK consume far in excess of this. The average intake is 3,200 mg per day which is thought to be too high. If we ate only unprocessed foods and added no salt to our food our intake would be very much less. About half our salt intake comes from processed foods such as white bread, cooked meats, cheese, soups, salted snack foods, sauces and gravies. If you need to reduce your salt intake, cut down on these foods as well as the amount of salt you use in cooking and add directly to your food. At first foods may taste quite bland, but other herbs and spices such as oregano, pepper, garlic, cumin and lemon juice are useful substitutes.

POTASSIUM

Like sodium, the major role of potassium relates to fluid balance within the body. A balance of sodium and potassium is essential for nerves to work correctly. The RNI for potassium in males and females over fourteen is 3,500 mg per day, with no increase set for pregnancy or breastfeeding. Potassium deficiency is perhaps more likely than sodium deficiency because we do not generally add it to foods, but deficiency is unusual (except occasionally after long bouts of diarrhoea and vomiting), because of its plentiful supply in foods. It is particularly abundant in vegetables and fruits, especially bananas. Milk, whole grains, legumes, fish and meats are also good sources.

Risk groups for deficiency of potassium include those suffering from anorexia nervosa or bulimia, people on very low calorie diets and heavily exercising athletes.

Table 15 in Appendix 2 lists rich sources of potassium.

CHLORIDE

Chloride also plays a vital role in the balance of the body's fluids, and in addition helps nerves work normally. The RNI for chloride is the same as for sodium, i.e. 1,600 mg per day, since their roles in the body are closely linked. Dietary intakes of sodium and chloride are usually very similar since salt is sodium and chloride in equal proportions. A few fruits and vegetables are naturally good sources of chloride, but most chloride is provided by the addition of salt to food.

MAGNESIUM

About 60 per cent of the body's magnesium is contained in the bones. The rest circulates in the blood and operates inside cells, where it is important for energy production. Magnesium deficiency can cause an irregular heartbeat and a low level of dietary intake may increase the risk of coronary heart disease. For women over eighteen years the RNI is 270 mg per day, for fifteen- to-eighteen-year-olds it is 300 mg per day. During pregnancy the extra requirements are usually met from the mother's body stores. During breastfeeding an extra intake of 50 mg per day is required.

Whole grains, seeds, nuts, pulses and fish are the richest sources of magnesium. Dairy products, meat and some vegetables are also good sources (see Table 16 in Appendix 2). 'Hard' tap water often contains high concentrations of magnesium. Over half the women in the recent national dietary survey consumed less than the RNI for magnesium, so do ensure that your diet contains plenty of magnesium-rich foods.

Trace Elements

Trace elements are minerals that are required in very small amounts by the body. Deficiency symptoms are listed in the following table.

Effect of trace element deficiency in adults

Trace element	Effect of dietary deficiency
Iron	Anaemia, general tiredness, low birthweight
Zinc	Lack of taste and smell, poor wound healing, skin rash, diarrhoea, loss of appetite, hair loss
Copper	Anaemia
Selenium	Muscle pain and weakness, heart muscle disease
Iodine	Thyroid gland problems
Fluoride	Increased risk of tooth decay
Chromium	Possible link with heart disease and diabetes

IRON

Iron is primarily needed for the formation of the protein haemoglobin in the red blood cells, which transport oxygen in the bloodstream. In pregnancy the number of red blood cells increases, which means that iron is a nutrient that is in great demand. Iron also forms part of the protein called myoglobin, which stores oxygen in muscles. Good stores of iron are essential for a healthy pregnancy. Many women, however, have very low stores of iron pre-pregnancy, due either to heavy blood loss during menstruation or inadequate iron intake, and supplemental iron is necessary during pregnancy to prevent anaemia (see page 131). The 1987 national dietary survey showed that iron intake was particularly likely to be deficient among women, with 50 per cent of women under thirty-five consuming less than 9.5 mg per day. To ensure that appropriate levels of iron are stored in the body, the RNI for menstruating women and girls has been set at 14.8 mg per day. Women with very high blood loss during their periods may need more than this. No increase is necessary during pregnancy because menstruation ceases, absorption of iron from the diet becomes more efficient and some of the body's stores of iron are brought into use.

There has also been no increase set in the RNI during breastfeeding; the small amount of iron needed in breast milk is generally offset by absent or infrequent menstruation.

Iron is present in many foods, both animal and plant, as you can see in Table 17 in Appendix 2, but note that dairy products are not a good source. The iron that is found in red meat is better absorbed than iron from other foods, so if you are vegetarian or vegan you need to take special care that your diet contains enough iron. Many vegan and vegetarian foods are fortified with iron.

There are steps you can take to increase the amount of iron you absorb from your food.

Steps to increase the amount of iron you absorb from your diet

1   Do not drink tea or coffee with iron-containing meals and snacks (or iron tablets) because the amount of iron that you absorb from that food will be reduced. Wait at least half an hour after eating before drinking tea and coffee.

2   Drinks or foods containing Vitamin C increase the amount of iron that you absorb from iron-containing foods. Good sources of Vitamin C are given in Table 13 in Appendix 2. Try always to have one of these with iron-containing foods.

3   Iron absorption is also reduced by eating whole grains and soya products which often form the basis of a meal for

vegetarians and vegans, who have already reduced their dietary iron intake by cutting out meat. Many soya products have iron added to them, so check before buying and always choose the fortified soya products if available.

ZINC

The mineral zinc is essential for many of the body's functions. It is particularly important for growth, wound healing and in the body's immune system, which protects against infection.

The RNI for zinc for all females over fourteen years is 7.0 mg per day. As with iron and calcium, although there is a recognized increased requirement for zinc during pregnancy, adaptations within the mother's body ensure an adequate supply to the developing baby, without the need for an increase in dietary zinc intake.

Additional zinc requirements during breastfeeding have been set at 6.0 mg per day for the first four months and 2.5 mg per day thereafter.

In general, protein-rich foods are also rich in zinc. Lean meats, poultry, eggs and dairy products are the best sources since the zinc in these foods is well absorbed. Good plant sources of zinc are whole grains, beans and nuts, but soil conditions can affect the amount present. Vegans need to take extra care that they have an adequate zinc intake. Table 18 in Appendix 3 will help you check this.

There is no evidence to suggest that intakes in excess of the RNI provide any extra benefit to the functioning of the immune system, and long term ingestion of high doses of zinc (75 mg per day or more) can lead to signs of copper deficiency. A high consumption of zinc has been shown to reduce both copper and iron asborption.

COPPER

Copper is important for iron absorption and in the formation of the body's supporting tissues. It also has several functions within the nervous system.

The RNI for copper for adults is 1.2 mg per day, with no increase for pregnancy, due to maternal adaptation. The increased requirement for breastfeeding is set at 0.3 mg per day. Good sources of copper are legumes (for example red kidney beans), nuts, meat and wholegrain bread. See also Table 19 in Appendix 3. Dairy products are a poor source.

Copper deficiency is very rare but research into the possible significance of copper deficiency in the UK, especially in relation to heart disease, is ongoing.

SELENIUM

Selenium is required for the healthy functioning of the body cells and works together with Vitamin E. An adequate intake of selenium reduces the requirement for Vitamin E. Current research is looking at whether adequate selenium intake may be important in cancer prevention.

The RNI for selenium is 60 mcg per day for females over fourteen years. Changes in the body's handling of selenium occur during pregnancy and no increase in intake is required. During breastfeeding an extra intake of 15 mcg per day is needed. Blood selenium levels in the UK suggest that current levels of selenium in our diets are adequate.

Good sources of selenium are Brazil nuts, fish, especially tuna, green and brown lentils, bread and milk. See Table 20 in Appendix 2.

IODINE

Iodine is an essential component of the hormones which are produced by the thyroid gland. If a person's iodine intake is inadequate, the thyroid gland enlarges as it attempts to take up more iodine from the bloodstream. A greatly enlarged thyroid gland is known as 'goitre', and the front of the neck looks very swollen. Iodine is necessary for the development of the baby's nervous system during the first three months of pregnancy. If a woman has an iodine-deficient diet during this time her baby may be born with short stature and develop mental retardation (known as cretinism). Iodine deficiency is extremely rare in the UK but it is still common in many areas of the world, including some parts of Europe. The RNI for iodine for females and males over fourteen years is 140 mcg per day. There is no increase set for pregnancy and breastfeeding. Major sources of iodine in the UK are enriched salt, dairy products and eggs. Fish is also an excellent source, for example haddock and kippers. See Table 21 in Appendix 2.

The average intake of iodine amongst women in the recent UK national survey was 176 mcg per day, therefore most women are easily consuming enough. Very high intakes can cause problems, however; 'toxic goitre', which has the same effect as iodine deficiency, has appeared in people consuming a lot of seaweed, but intakes of up to six times the RNI appear to be safe, so this should not be a worry.

FLUORIDE

Fluoride helps to strengthen developing teeth so that they are more resistant to decay. It is also incorporated into developing bones, but it is not known whether it is actually essential for growth in humans.

There is no RNI for fluoride, but the Department of Health recommends that water supplies are fluoridated to achieve levels of 1 mg per kg (1 part per million or 1 ppm), because of the ability of fluoride at this concentration to reduce tooth decay in children by about 50 per cent. Tea, seafoods and some natural water sources are the only good dietary sources of fluoride. Excessive fluoride can cause mottling of the teeth (small spots of discoloration).

CHROMIUM

Chromium is important for the conversion of glucose into energy, and deficiency of it may be related to diabetes and coronary heart disease.

Good sources of chromium include egg yolks, meat, yeast, whole grains, legumes and nuts. Highly refined foods are low in chromium.

No RNI has been set for chromium but a safe and adequate level of intake is thought to be at least 25 mg per day for adults.

MANGANESE

The mineral manganese (not to be confused with magnesium) plays a part in the breakdown of carbohydrate for energy and it is also important in bone formation. Our needs for manganese are, however, very low (adequate intakes are thought to be about 1.4 mg per day for adults) and our diets tend to be fairly rich in this mineral (average intakes among women have been observed to be about 3.3 mg per day). Deficiency among humans is almost unknown.

Whole grains, nuts, beans and leafy green vegetables are good sources of manganese.

MOLYBDENUM

Molybdenum is another nutrient required in minute amounts for some specific body activities. Deficiency has never been observed in people consuming a normal diet. Safe intakes are thought to be between 50 and 400 mcg per day and good sources include whole grains, beans and nuts.

Other minerals found in the body

No other minerals found within the body, such as aluminium, lead, cadmium, mercury, have been demonstrated to be essential, and some in fact may be contaminants of the body and harmful above certain levels.

NUTRIENTS THAT MAY OFFER PROTECTION AGAINST ILLNESS WHETHER YOU ARE PREGNANT OR NOT

A huge amount of money is being spent in many different countries to try to find out why some populations have much higher incidences of diseases such as cancer and heart disease than others. There is increasing evidence that the key lies in the different consumption of fruit and vegetables (especially raw varieties). The precise component of fruit and vegetables that contains the protective factor has not been identified, but there are two very strong candidates: a group of vitamins and minerals known as the antioxidant vitamins and minerals, and the essential fatty acid alpha-linolenic acid (see page 56 for good dietary sources).

The antioxidant or ACE vitamins are:

Vitamin A in the form of carotene (the plant form of Vitamin A for which there is no recommended upper limit in pregnancy, unlike retinol, the form of Vitamin A derived from animals, see page 17), especially beta-carotene, which is found mainly in the yellow-, orange- and red-coloured fruit and vegetables.

Vitamin C or ascorbic acid, which is found in fruit and vegetables, especially citrus fruits (see Table 13 in Appendix 2 for the best sources).

Vitamin E, for which the best sources are seeds, nuts and vegetable oils.

There is increasing evidence that the ACE or antioxidant vitamins, together with the antioxidant minerals selenium, zinc, copper and manganese, if taken in sufficient quantities, by eating plenty of fruit and vegetables, protect our bodies against disease, particularly cancer and heart disease. Recent research has shown that the ACE vitamins and minerals may also offer protection against common illnesses such as colds, improve the quality of men's sperm, reduce the incidence and severity of symptoms associated with PIH (pregnancy-induced hypertension, see page 133), and reduce the problems endured by arthritis sufferers.

The antioxidant nutrients mainly protect the fat component of body cells and membranes from damage caused by agents known as free-radicals. The easiest way to understand the principle is to think of a slab of butter that has been left in a warm room for a long period. The butter becomes rancid, which means that its chemical structure has been altered by the presence of oxygen (from the air) and heat, resulting in, amongst other things, an alteration of flavour. Think of the antioxidant nutrients as protecting your body cells and membranes from 'becoming rancid'. So read the advice in Chapter 4 and try to ensure that you and your family eat at least five portions of fruit and vegetables each day.

CHAPTER FOUR

Foods that Supply the Essential Nutrients

In order for your diet to provide all the nutrients that you need you should include a wide range of foods. Most foods contain a variety of nutrients but all are deficient in one or more. Ensuring that your body gets everything it needs to work effectively and efficiently may appear very difficult and complicated but there is an easy, almost foolproof, method of making sure that your diet provides all essential nutrients by using the UK National Food Guide which is the 'Balance of Good Health' plate.

THE 'BALANCE OF GOOD HEALTH' PLATE

The diagram of a plate of food shown on page 82 is divided into sections which correspond to the contribution that the particular food group should make towards your daily diet.

The food groups are:

Bread, other cereals and potatoes (commonly known as starchy foods)
Fruit and vegetables
Meat, fish and alternatives (commonly known as protein foods)
Milk and dairy foods (commonly known as high calcium foods)
Fatty and sugary foods

As you can see from the 'Balance of Good Health' plate, the bread, other cereals and potatoes group together with the fruit and vegetables group are particularly important and should be

	Starchy foods	Fruit & vegetables	Protein foods	Calcium foods	Fatty and sugary foods
Women planning a pregnancy	8*	9*	2–3*	2–3*	Use sparingly
Pregnant women					
1–6 months	8	9	2–3	3	"
7–9 months	10	9	2–3	3	"
Breastfeeding women					
< 2 months	11	11	2–3	5	"
2–4 months	12	11	2–3	5	"
4–6 months	12	11	2–3	5	"
> 6 months	12	11	2–3	5	"

* Servings per day

the basis of all your meals and snacks, in addition to small amounts of the meat, fish and alternatives group and the milk and dairy foods group. Foods from the fatty and sugary foods group should be restricted.

The chart above shows you how many servings of each group you need each day (the tables in Appendix 2 indicate what is meant by a serving). The recommended number of servings applies to a woman of average weight and physical activity. Later in this chapter you will also be advised about how to adapt the 'Balance of Good Health' plate to your particular situation.

Starchy Foods – Group 1

These foods consist of breads, cereals, rice, pasta, noodles and potatoes. They are the foundation of a healthy diet since they are good sources of carbohydrates, protein and B vitamins as well as being filling and relatively cheap.

In their natural state they contain very little natural fat, but it is easy to eat them in a high fat way, for example by eating chips instead of boiled/jacket potatoes, by adding large amounts of butter or cheese to your bread, or by using full fat creamy milk on your breakfast cereal or to make sauces.

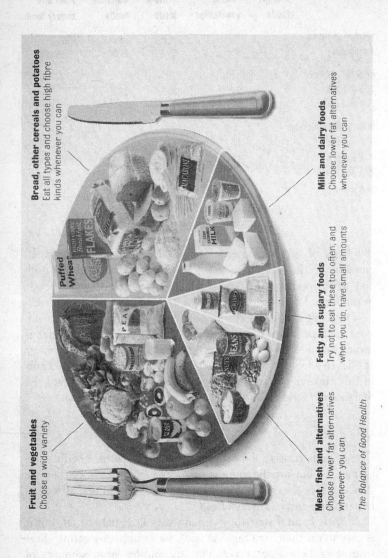

Bread, other cereals and potatoes
Eat all types and choose high fibre kinds whenever you can

Milk and dairy foods
Choose lower fat alternatives whenever you can

Fatty and sugary foods
Try not to eat these too often, and when you do, have small amounts

Fruit and vegetables
Choose a wide variety

Meat, fish and alternatives
Choose lower fat alternatives whenever you can

The Balance of Good Health

Starchy foods can be a very valuable source of dietary fibre (roughage), which has an important role in preventing constipation, but only if you eat the wholegrain varieties such as wholemeal bread, wholegrain breakfast cereals or pasta and brown rice. If you do not like wholemeal bread try some of the new softgrain breads, which are made with white flour but have fibre added back. Wholegrain cereals are important sources of thiamin, riboflavin and niacin. Some breads and breakfast cereals also have folic acid added to them. Oats are particularly rich in another type of fibre called soluble fibre (also found in some fruits and vegetables, and pulses), which can help to prevent heart disease and diabetes. Try adding oats to different sweet and savoury dishes, for example to soups, sauces and stews or to crumbles, yoghurt, or dried fruit.

If you like them, have a breakfast cereal most days because many have minerals, such as iron and calcium, and vitamins added to them.

The table on page 81 recommends an average of 9 servings of the starchy foods each day. If you are trying to lose weight before or after pregnancy, or trying to restrict your weight gain during pregnancy, don't think that you should cut down your daily intake of these starchy foods – it is the sugary and fatty foods that should be avoided (see page 86–8).

One serving of starchy food is equivalent to a slice of bread, a small bowl of cereal, a small helping of rice, pasta or noodles, or two egg-sized potatoes.

Fruit and Vegetables – Group 2

Remember the old saying 'an apple a day keeps the doctor away'? The foods in this group form the second group of the plate and you should aim to eat 9 servings of fruit, fruit juice and vegetables/salads each day and don't forget to include some of the dark green and orange vegetables, and orange-coloured fruit. Fruit and vegetables provide many important nutrients and much dietary fibre or roughage for pregnancy and breastfeeding.

You can enjoy a wide variety of different fresh fruits and

vegetables all the year round, but buying them in season is usually cheaper. The most important vitamins provided by fruit and vegetables are Vitamin C, carotene (the plant form of vitamin A) and some of the B group, i.e. thiamin, riboflavin, niacin, pyridoxine and folic acid. Some of these important vitamins are not very stable and it is easy to destroy them during food storage, processing or cooking. Vitamin C and carotene are also known as ACE or antioxidant vitamins and are thought to have an import-ant role in protecting your body against diseases such as heart disease and cancer (see page 78 for more information). Try to reduce these vitamin losses by remembering the following points when shopping and cooking.

- Frozen vegetables and fruit provide as many vitamins as fresh varieties, but drying and canning them reduces the vitamin content.
- Do not store fresh fruit and vegetables for long time – storage reduces the vitamin content, so eat them as soon after purchase as possible.
- Try to eat some raw fruit and vegetables each day – particularly the orange-coloured fruit and vegetables – as they have more vitamins than cooked ones.
- Some of the vitamins in fruit and vegetables dissolve into the cooking water, so always cook them in the minimum amount of boiling water and try to then use this water for gravies, etc. Steamed and microwaved fruit and vegetables have more vitamins than boiled ones.
- Eat fruit and vegetables as soon as possible after cooking since keeping them warm for a long time also reduces the vitamin content.
- Avoid preparing and keeping vegetables and fruit under water in advance of cooking. Again the vitamins will dissolve into the water.

Fruit and vegetable juices are a form of processed fruit and vegetables and although they still provide vitamins and minerals, they lack important dietary fibre.

Milk, yoghurt and cheese – Group 3

The foods in Group 3 are particularly high in calcium and you should aim for 2–3 servings each day. A serving consists of half a pint of milk, a small pot of yoghurt, or about 40 g (1½ oz) hard Cheddar-type cheese. If you are vegetarian/vegan or have an allergy to dairy foods, check Table 14 in Appendix 2 for alternative sources of calcium. If you are trying to cut down your calorie intake, there are many low fat varieties of milk, cheese and yoghurt available (such as skimmed or semi-skimmed milk, half fat cheese, low fat yoghurts) which still provide as much essential calcium as their high fat alternatives. Exposing milk to sunlight, for example leaving milk on the doorstep all day, will significantly reduce the vitamin riboflavin content, so always store milk in a dark place. UHT or ultraheat treatment significantly reduces some of the essential vitamins found in milk, so use fresh milk whenever possible.

Protein Foods – Group 4

Foods from this group, which includes meat, poultry, fish, pulses (peas, beans and lentils), eggs and nuts, make up the third portion of the food plate. They are a major source of protein (which is also found in cereals and vegetables) as well as vitamins and minerals. Proteins are made up of small building blocks called amino acids, some of which your body can make itself, and some, called essential amino acids, which must be supplied in a regular amount by your diet. Protein from animal sources contains all the essential amino acids but some vegetable proteins may be short in one or more of these amino acids. This does not mean that it is only by eating animal protein that you will be getting everything that you need, since vegetable proteins, if eaten in the correct combinations, will satisfy all your requirements. For example, the amino acid that is low in grain foods, such as rice and wheat, is found in high amounts in pulses. Therefore eating beans on toast, or rice with soya beans gives an excellent combined protein count. Grains and pulses will always balance each other.

A serving of protein is equivalent to 55 g (2 oz) lean meat, poultry or oily fish, 85 g (3 oz) white fish, two eggs or 275 g (10 oz) of pulses (cooked weight). Two to three servings per day is sufficient – there is no benefit from a high protein diet. The amount of extra protein needed for pregnancy is equivalent to that found in 28 g (1 oz) meat, or 40 g (1½ oz) fish, or one egg, or 140 g (5 oz) pulses (cooked weight), or 28 g (1 oz) nuts, or 3 average slices of bread, so you can see not much extra is needed.

Although protein foods are very important, some of them, particularly those from animal sources such as meat, can also contribute too much fat to your diet – particularly saturated fat, which can increase your risk of developing heart disease. Check the advice below which shows you how to cut down your dietary fat intake.

Fatty and sugary foods – Group 5

FATTY FOODS

Fats and oils occur naturally in many foods, including meat, oily fish, dairy foods, nuts and seeds, in addition to the fats and oils that are added to food during and after cooking. Fats and oils provide important nutrients, particularly the essential fatty acids linoleic acid and linolenic acid. The majority of people in the UK eat too much fat, especially animal fat. Listed below are some examples of how to cut down the total fat and saturated fat content of your diet.

- Removing the visible fat from a pork chop reduces its fat content by about 50 per cent.
- The fat content of a chicken portion is reduced by 60 per cent if the skin is removed.
- Grilling bacon rather than frying reduces its fat content by 17 per cent. Fine cut frozen chips contain 21 per cent fat

after frying compared with the 4 per cent of oven chips after baking, and the 7 per cent fat of home-made chips.

- Fried fish in batter or breadcrumbs contains seven to ten times as much fat as steamed or baked fish without the coating.
- Low fat products and semi-skimmed milk generally contain about half the fat. Skimmed milk contains virtually no fat at all.
- Most sandwich fillings and spreads taste just as good without the customary layer of butter or margarine. You will decrease the fat content of, for example, a ham and pickle sandwich by 35 per cent by eating it in this way.
- Don't eat too many processed foods with a high fat content, for example sausages (25 per cent fat), beefburgers (17 per cent fat) and other meat products such as pork pies, Cornish pasties and sausage rolls (36 per cent fat), crisps and other savoury snacks (30 per cent or more fat) and cakes, biscuits and pastries (usually about 20–30 per cent fat).
- Lean red meat contains at least 10 per cent fat, chicken (without skin) about 5 per cent, but most legumes, such as lentils and beans, contain less than 1 per cent fat.
- Cheescake (33 per cent fat), milk pudding (20 per cent fat) and ice cream (24 per cent fat) are great as occasional treats, but you can considerably reduce your average 'after dinner' fat intake by usually eating fruit or low fat yoghurt which contains less than 1 per cent fat.

SUGARY FOOD

Sugar is found naturally in many foods such as fruit, vegetables and milk. Many people believe that they need a constant supply of processed or added sugars to give them energy, for example sugar added to tea or coffee, fizzy drinks and squashes, sweets, biscuits, cakes, chocolate and breakfast cereals. However, starchy food from cereals, potatoes, pulses and some vegetables is broken down in your body to make sugar which provides all the energy that you need.

Added sugar, whether brown or white, provides empty calories. In other words there are no vitamins or minerals provided as well, whereas the breakdown of starchy foods or fruit and milk to produce sugar also generates vitamins and minerals. Often all that added sugar contributes to is tooth decay and obesity. Many people have been heard to say, 'I don't eat much sugar' meaning that they don't add sugar to drinks or cereals, but they perhaps forget how much sugar is added by manufacturers during food processing. Check the labels of foods – many manufacturers now state how much sugar they have added, but if they don't, check the ingredients list. The nearer an ingredient is to the beginning of the list, the more there is of it in that product – for example, if sugar appears second in a list of ingredients then you can assume there is a lot of it in that product, whereas if sugar appears second to last you can assume there is very little of it. Don't forget that there are many different names for added sugars including glucose, sucrose, maltose and dextrose.

Don't think that you should avoid all sweet foods though. Most people enjoy chocolate and sweets and sticky puddings, but you should save them for treats rather than having them every day. There are also many good-quality low sugar or sugar-free drinks available such as low calorie squash and diet fizzy drinks, and by changing to these brands you can significantly reduce your added sugar intake. There is no evidence that the artificial sweeteners that these products contain are harmful during pregnancy (see page 117 for more information).

VEGETARIANISM

In Britain people choose to be vegetarian or vegan for religious, cultural or personal reasons, yet in many parts of the world vegetarianism is mandatory and not a choice. If a vegetarian/vegan diet is planned carefully there is no reason why it should be unhealthy or lacking in essential nutrients. In fact vegetarians/vegans tend to suffer less from 'the diseases of affluence', i.e. diabetes, heart disease and hypertension, than others in the general population. It also appears that vegetarian women, even strict vegans, have only the same incidence of problems with their periods or fertility as omnivorous women, i.e. women who eat animal foods. The only reason why vegetarian/vegan women may experience menstrual problems is if their diet causes their weight to drop too low.

There are various classifications of vegetarians:

1   Vegans – only eat food of plant origin, i.e. they do not eat meat, fish, dairy foods or eggs or any products made from them, e.g. lard, suet.
2   Lacto-vegetarians – eat plant foods and dairy foods such as milk and cheese.
3   Lacto-ovo-vegetarians – eat plant foods, dairy foods and eggs.
4   Partial vegetarians – eat plant foods, dairy foods, eggs and fish, i.e. they avoid only meat and poultry.

It cannot be emphasized too strongly that a vegetarian diet is healthy only if the nutrients excluded by avoiding animal or dairy foods are replaced from vegetable sources. Below are some guidelines about nutrients in which vegetarians/vegans are at risk of becoming deficient. An excellent book on vegetarianism during pregnancy and after the birth containing many easy-to-follow recipes is Rose Elliot's *Mother and Baby Book*, published by Harper Collins.

PROTEIN

Vegetarians/vegans who do not eat animal protein are at a higher risk of being deficient in one of the building blocks used to manufacture proteins in your body for new cells, tissues and hormones for you and your baby. The answer is to mix plant foods together so that the protein building blocks balance each other. If one food is short of a building block it should be combined with another food that has an excess of that building block. Examples of plant protein sources that should be combined are cereals (such as rice, wheat and corn) and pulses (such as beans and peas), for example beans on toast or rice with lentils. (See Appendix 1 for meal plans and recipes.) Other protein sources that should be included in a vegetarian/vegan diet are nuts, seeds, plant milks and textured vegetable protein and tofu cheese. Check Table 4 in Appendix 2 to see how many portions are recommended for pregnancy planning, during pregnancy and breastfeeding.

CALCIUM

Calcium is needed for strong bones and teeth. Dairy foods are good sources and calcium in this form is very well absorbed. If you do not eat dairy foods then you should be careful about ensuring that your diet has enough calcium. Check the table on page 81 to ensure that you have the correct number of servings from the calcium group and Table 14 in Appendix 2 showing the amount of calcium in different foods.

IRON

The most easily absorbed form of iron is found only in animal foods, but vegetarians/vegans can easily achieve an adequate dietary iron intake from plant foods such as apricots, peaches, whole grains, pulses and seeds (see Table 17 in Appendix 2 for more information). It is also important to remember that a meal with a high Vitamin C content will increase the amount of iron absorbed from that meal. Many foods are now fortified with iron, for example most breakfast cereals, and some brands of bread, and foods commonly eaten by vegetarians/vegans, for example soya milk and tofu cheese.

ZINC

Although concern has been expressed about the zinc content of vegetarian/vegan diets, this is not because the diet is low in zinc but because the diet is usually high in fibre, which is associated with a high phytate content. Phytate can inhibit zinc absorption. However, studies have shown that there is no difference in the blood zinc levels between vegetarian/vegan and omnivorous pregnant women (see Table 18 in Appendix 2 for good dietary sources of zinc).

COBALAMIN (VITAMIN B12)

Vitamin B12 or cobalamin does not naturally occur in a strict vegetarian/vegan diet. However, many foods are fortified with it, including yeast extracts such as Marmite, Barmine, some soya milks and vegetarian cheese and spreads. Check Table 12 in Appendix 2 for more information about food sources.

TEENAGERS

For women aged from thirteen to nineteen years it is not their actual age that has the greatest influence on their pregnancy outcome but the number of years between the onset of their periods and pregnancy. The shorter this interval the greater the potential for nutritional deficiencies, particularly if the interval is three years or less. Nutritional deficiencies are more likely during pregnancy in these younger girls because:

- They need enough nutrients to complete their own growth as well as to fulfil the demands of a growing baby.
- They are more likely to try to conceal the pregnancy and often deny themselves foods to restrict pregnancy weight gain and prevent the pregnancy 'showing'.
- Teenage girls are more likely than older women to eat irregular meals, to have bizarre eating habits, to miss meals, particularly breakfast, to include a large number of fast foods and be greatly influenced by pressure from food advertisers and their peers.
- Pregnant teenagers often feel socially isolated, for example because they have had to leave home or school or work, or because they cannot participate in typical teenage social activities. Social and economic influences have an important effect on eating behaviour.

Pregnant teenage girls (as well as teenagers in general) should take extra care with their diets and it is never too late to start following the healthy eating guidelines in this book. Teenage girls need to be particularly careful about their calcium and iron intakes.

WOMEN WHO ARE TRYING TO LOSE WEIGHT OR RESTRICT THEIR PREGNANCY WEIGHT GAIN

It has already been emphasized in Chapter 1 that being very overweight increases the risk of having a poor pregnancy outcome. The time to lose weight is before becoming pregnant, not whilst pregnant. However, some pregnant women may be advised to restrict the rate of weight gain during pregnancy and need to follow the advice below but not so strictly that they actually lose body weight (see Chapter 2 for more advice about weight gain). Most women at the end of pregnancy end up with a few pounds or kgs excess fat. They are very keen to lose this weight, but remember, it has taken nine months to put on and it will not disappear overnight. Breastfeeding women can lose weight, but it should be done very gradually so they do not end up feeling tired.

Advising overweight women who are planning a pregnancy, pregnant women who need to restrict their weight gain and breast- and bottle-feeding women who want to lose weight is very difficult because all these women will need different amounts of energy or calories. The advice below is therefore very general. If you need more detailed or specific advice, consult your practice nurse/midwife/GP, who may be able to help or may refer you to a dietitian. Alternatively, there are some very good support groups to help with weight loss.

General advice for restricting calorie (energy) intake to lose weight

Follow the chart on page 81 about the number of servings you need from each of the food groups in the food plate, whether you are planning a pregnancy, pregnant or breastfeeding. By reducing the fat and sugar content of many of these foods it is possible to reduce the calorie (energy) content without going hungry or reducing your intake of valuable nutrients.

STARCHY FOODS – GROUP 1

Starchy foods are often thought of as 'fattening foods' but they are not particularly high in calories and are very filling, particularly the wholegrain varieties. But it is easy to eat them in a high calorie way by adding fat and sugar to them, for example by:

- eating chips instead of boiled or jacket potatoes
- putting a lot of butter or margarine on to bread
- eating fried rice, or adding rich creamy sauces to pasta and noodles
- adding full fat milk and sugar to breakfast cereals
- eating breakfast cereals with a high sugar content

Eat starchy foods without adding a lot of fat and sugar.

FRUIT AND VEGETABLES – GROUP 2

Fruit and vegetables contain mainly water and very few calories. Again, by reducing the fat and sugar added to them, it is possible to reduce their calorie content.

- Choose fruit that is either fresh, stewed without sugar or tinned in natural juice rather than a heavy syrup.
- Vegetables should be eaten raw or cooked in water rather than fried or with rich creamy sauces added to them.

MEAT, FISH, PULSES, EGGS AND NUTS – GROUP 3

Again it is possible to eat these foods in a low fat way.

- Meat should be lean with all visible fat removed.
- Cook without the addition of fat, for example by grilling or baking instead of frying.
- Fat should be skimmed off meat stews and casseroles and from the juices provided by roasting meat.
- Do not eat the skin on poultry – it is very high in fat.
- Meat products such as sausages, beefburgers and some pâtés and cold meats can have a high fat and high calorie content – try to choose low fat varieties.
- Avoid meat, fish or chicken coated in batter or breadcrumbs and fried. Also any of the above cooked in pastry, for example sausage rolls, meat, fish or chicken pies, should be avoided.
- Use vegetables and herbs to flavour bean and nut dishes so that very little fat is needed to cook and flavour these foods.

MILK, CHEESE AND YOGHURT – GROUP 4

Dairy foods have a high fat content but there are many excellent low fat alternatives available. In nearly all cases it is only the fat (and calories) that are reduced and not nutrients.

- Try skimmed or semi-skimmed milk instead of the full fat varieties.
- Use half fat Cheddar-type cheeses and low fat cream or spread cheeses.
- Low fat yoghurt both natural and flavoured is available, also watch the sugar content of fruit and flavoured yoghurts.

When trying to lose weight you should be particularly careful about your fat intake because fat is the most energy (calorie) dense nutrient. The previous pages give advice about how to reduce the fat you obtain from protein and dairy foods and pages 86 and 87 provide information on reducing fat intake generally.

Reducing your intake of sugary food as described on page 88 will also help you to lose weight.

EATING ON A BUDGET

There are many reasons why money for food may be limited, for example unemployment, low pay, existing children needing clothes and shoes, high mortgages, the impact of two salaries being reduced to one and probably most importantly living on benefits.

Women often bear the brunt of there not being enough food to go around by cutting their own intake to make sure there is enough for their partners and children. Women on low incomes are more likely to have low birthweight babies and/or babies who are ill in the newborn period. Dietary surveys have shown that people on low incomes eat more fatty and sugary food and less fruit, vegetables and dietary fibre than people on higher incomes.

The benefit system in the UK changes regularly and depends on age and social circumstances so it is not possible to give accurate information about extra help on offer to pregnant and breastfeeding women. However, most antenatal clinics have medical social workers available who can give advice, or visit your local advice centre (Appendix 3 also has some useful addresses of support groups).

It is possible to eat a healthy diet whilst on a low income but it can be difficult. It involves a great deal of time and effort to shop around for bargains and cook cheap, nourishing meals. Below are some tips to make the budget go further and advice on cheap, healthy meals and recipes is given in Appendix 1 (pages 174 to 178).

- Try to work out a rough plan of what you are going to eat over the next few days, then make a shopping list to avoid impulse buys.
- To avoid waste, buy foods only in quantities you know you will use.
- Choose supermarket own brands as they tend to be cheaper than the labelled brands and look out for special offers. When comparing brands check the weight you get for the price.
- Look out for reduced price items that are near their sell-by date, but don't use any foods that are past their use-by date.
- Shop around to find the best prices and use markets if available.
- Buy fruit and vegetables in season.

ETHNIC DIETS

The following few pages give advice regarding dietary practices and customs of some of the major UK non-Caucasian ethnic groups, particularly in relation to pregnancy and whilst breastfeeding.

Asian women originating from the Indian subcontinent

Hindus If you are a Hindu you are likely to be a strict vegetarian and may also fast for one or two days per week. It is not advisable for pregnant and breastfeeding women to fast because the large fluctuations in your metabolism may affect the developing baby or your production of breast milk. Vegetarians need to check that their diet includes sufficient quantities of essential nutrients which are more abundant in animal products, such as calcium, iron, vitamins B12 and D (see below and pages 88 to 91 for further information).

Muslims Rigorous fasting during the month of Ramadan should not be undertaken by pregnant and breastfeeding women because the alterations in your body's metabolism may be detrimental to the developing baby or may affect your production of breast milk.

Sikhs If you are vegetarian, check that you are eating foods that contain sufficient quantities of the nutrients which are more common in animal foods and are particularly important during pregnancy (see below and pages 88 to 91). It is also not advisable to fast whilst pregnant and breastfeeding because the fluctuations this will cause in your body's nutrient metabolism may not be good for the developing baby and may affect your production of breast milk.

Potential dietary deficiencies for Asian women originating from the Indian subcontinent

Calcium Traditional Asian diets are often low in calcium with dairy foods especially not being eaten in large amounts. Asian diets are also often high in wholewheat cereals (such as wholewheat chapati flour), which are also high in phytate, which inhibits calcium absorption. Table 14 in Appendix 2 listing dietary calcium sources should be carefully checked to make sure an adequate supply is eaten. Pregnant and breastfeeding Asian women may be advised to take calcium supplements.

Vitamin D The typical Asian diet does not provide much Vitamin D and many Asian women, particulary Muslim women, cover their head and body and therefore do not manufacture much Vitamin D in their skin. It is recommended that pregnant and breastfeeding Asian women take a supplement of 10 mcg of Vitamin D and also include good dietary sources of the vitamin (see Table 6 in Appendix 2).

Iron Because many Asian women are vegetarian their diet may be low in iron and the iron from typical Asian foods is not well absorbed. Table 17 in Appendix 2 lists good dietary iron sources, and page 72 gives advice on how to increase iron absorption.

Chinese Women

If you follow the traditional diet based on small amounts of meat and fish with large amounts of vegetables and rice or noodles, your diet is likely to be healthy. Diet plays an important part in good health according to Chinese medicine, by helping to maintain the balance of the two opposite elements in the body, 'yin' and 'yang'. In illness, the body becomes too 'hot' (an excess of yang) or too 'cold' (an excess of yin). Pregnancy is thought to be a 'hot' condition so this may mean you are cutting down on 'hot' foods such as oily fish, red meat, certain spices and some fruits such as mango and pineapple. Then for several weeks after the birth of your baby you may be encouraged to eat 'hot' foods again to regain your strength. If you do avoid certain 'hot' or 'cold' foods during pregnancy, check the advice earlier in this chapter and the nutrient tables in Appendix 2 to ensure that you can replace any essential nutrients that you may be excluding.

Vietnamese Women

Your diet and any changes you make during pregnancy may be similar to those described in the section for Chinese women above (i.e. based on the 'yin' and 'yang' concepts). If so, and you are avoiding certain 'hot' or 'cold' foods at different times, do check that you are not falling short of any essential nutrients by referring to the advice earlier in this chapter and the nutrient charts in Appendix 2. It is possible that calcium in particular may be low in your diet since rice grown in Vietnam contains much more calcium than the rice imported into Britain. Also fruit and vegetables in the UK contain less calcium than some tropical varieties and milk and cheese (the major dietary calcium sources) may not form a significant part of your diet. So check the dietary calcium advice on page 67 and use Table 14 in Appendix 2 to ensure that you are having enough.

Rastafarian Women

The Rastafarian dietary regime can be quite restrictive and, if yours is so, you do need to follow the dietary guidelines outlined in this chapter carefully and check your intake of essential nutrients (see tables in Appendix 2 and refer to Chapter 3). It is reported that Rastafarian women often have their children at a fairly young age with short intervals between pregnancies. This may lead to nutritional depletion, particularly of iron, folate and vitamin B12, which can cause anaemia, so do check these nutrients particularly.

Jewish Women

Jewish dietary rules should not pose any particular problems during pregnancy or breastfeeding, but fasting during Jewish festival days is best avoided, since the metabolic fluctuations that occur during fasting may not be good for the developing baby.

CHAPTER FIVE

Food Safety
and Foods to Avoid

ALCOHOL

The less alcohol you drink when you are pregnant or actively planning to conceive the better, because alcohol passes via the placenta and directly affects the baby. Women who drink large amounts of alcohol will obtain a high proportion of their daily calorie (energy) intake from it. These calories are referred to as empty calories because they do not have many nutrients associated with them and heavy drinkers often have B Vitamin (especially folic acid), zinc and magnesium deficiency.

However, for centuries women have been drinking and producing healthy babies, so is there a safe level of alcohol intake for pregnancy? When looking at the effects of alcohol it is necessary to consider various factors, including how much is taken in any one day and how often. There may be a difference between regular intakes and binge drinking.

Alcohol is generally described in units:

1 unit alcohol = 10 g alcohol
1 unit alcohol = 1 pub measure of spirits
1 unit alcohol = ½ pint ordinary strength beer/lager
1 unit alcohol = 1 glass red or white wine

For women in the UK who are not pregnant the Health Education Authority recommends an upper limit of 14 units of alcohol per week, spread throughout the week, with one or two drink-free days. For men the recommended upper limit is 21 units per week. The reason for the difference is that the effect of a given amount of alcohol is greater in women than men; in other words, women cannot process alcohol as well as men, mainly because of the disparity in their body weight.

Research studies have been designed to answer the question of how much alcohol women can safely take during pregnancy. The results are conflicting. The effect of alcohol is greater in women who smoke, drink large amounts of caffeine-containing drinks and have a poor diet. The available evidence is that there should be an upper limit of 8 units of alcohol per week for a pregnant woman and she should not take more than 2 units of alcohol in any one day. Women who drink more than 6 units per day have a high chance of producing a baby with fetal alcohol syndrome (see below). There is no evidence of harm from drinking less than 2 units per day, although many women choose to give up alcohol altogether. For those drinking between 2 and 6 units there is a risk of fetal alcohol effects, which although milder than fetal alcohol syndrome are still harmful.

If you are actively planning a pregnancy it is advisable to follow the recommendation for pregnant women, that is a maximum of 8 units of alcohol per week. The same advice also applies when you are breastfeeding because alcohol passes to the baby via the breast milk.

The effect on the baby of heavy drinking

Babies born to women who are chronic alcoholics or drink very heavily (i.e. more than 6 units per day) have a distinctive set of handicapping characteristics which is known as fetal alcohol syndrome or FAS.

CHARACTERISTICS OF FETAL ALCOHOL SYNDROME

Facial handicaps
>   low nasal bridge
>   short nose
>   small eyes
>   large space between eyes

　　long area between the nose and lips
　　thin upper lip
　　flat midface
　　minor ear abnormalities

Growth handicaps
　　infants are shorter and weigh less than expected

Handicaps affecting the brain
　　poor co-ordination
　　below average intelligence
　　hyperactivity
　　learning difficulties
　　attention problems
　　delayed development

A lot of babies of mothers who drink heavily do not survive. Those who do are irritable and hyperactive because of alcohol withdrawal. They also fail to grow normally and have poor rates of weight gain.

CAFFEINE

Caffeine is found in coffee, tea, cocoa and cola-type beverages. The reason why concern is expressed about it is because it acts like a mild stimulant and when you are pregnant this effect will also be exerted on your baby.

In the early 1980s research emerged showing that pregnant rats taking excess caffeine were more likely to give birth to offspring with handicaps. Several very large studies have failed to show these effects in human babies. Similarly, studies on maternal caffeine intake and the risk of miscarriage have failed to give conclusive results.

There is some evidence to suggest that if pregnant women consume largish amounts of alcohol, the effect of that alcohol on the baby is increased if the mother also drinks a lot of coffee. What is also evident, however, is that women who take a large amount of alcohol and caffeine are also less likely to have a very nutritious diet. Sometimes it is difficult to isolate which of the three – alcohol, excess coffee or a poor diet – is really responsible. The available research evidence is that pregnant women who have no more than five cups of ordinary strength coffee per day (which is equivalent to 10 cups of tea or cocoa or 12 glasses of cola) have no higher risk of miscarriage or other pregnancy problems than women who do.

Again, the above advice also applies if you are trying to conceive or are breastfeeding.

LIVER

The United Kingdom Department of Health advised in 1990 (and the advice was reinforced in 1993) that all pregnant women, and women planning a pregnancy, should avoid liver and liver products such as liver pâté and liver sausage because they contain very high levels of the retinol form of Vitamin A. Vitamin A is supplied to the body in two forms: retinol, which is present in animal and fish food sources, and carotene, which is found in plant sources. You need only be careful about having high intakes of the retinol form of Vitamin A.

If pregnant women consume excessive amounts of retinol, i.e. more than 3,300 mcg per day (which is four times greater than the recommended amount), around the time of conception and during the first three months, there is an increased risk of their babies being born with handicaps. Retinol is given to animals to promote growth and any excess in their bodies is stored in their liver, which is why a portion of animal liver may contain between 12 and 20 times the recommended dietary intake. It is important to remember that babies will only be affected by handicaps if their mothers have had very high retinol intakes every day. It is very, very unlikely that if you have an odd portion of liver early in pregnancy your baby will be affected. In fact, there have not been any reported incidences in the UK of babies being affected by their mothers eating liver in early pregnancy.

FOOD-RELATED INFECTIONS

The advice on the following pages about avoiding the infections listeriosis, toxoplasmosis, salmonellosis, chlamydiosis and other food-borne infections is very important. BUT do not become so concerned that you are frightened to eat any food that has not been bought and prepared by yourself. That is, don't be afraid to eat out at restaurants or at friends' houses. The incidence of these infections in pregnancy is very low when compared to the number of pregnancies in the UK each year. So just be sensible and not obsessive about the food safety advice or you will end up a nervous wreck.

But if you do become worried that you may have eaten or drunk something inadvisable, go and see your midwife or doctor or ring the Eating for Pregnancy Helpline on 0114 2424084 to discuss the likelihood of you having been infected. Don't wait at home and worry.

This next section is aimed mainly at women who are already pregnant. However, if you are planning a pregnancy it is also sensible to follow the advice. Women who are breastfeeding do not need to follow the special advice about listeriosis, toxoplasmosis, or chlamydiosis, or keep to the guidelines about sheep and cats because these infections are not passed by mothers to their babies via breast milk.

Listeriosis

The correct name for this bacterium is listeria monocytogenes. It is present all around us in soil, water and vegetation and causes problems only in people whose immune system (their defence against infection) is not working properly. This includes pregnant women, people undergoing chemotherapy, those who have recently had organ or bone marrow transplants, or those who have AIDS (acquired immune deficiency syndrome).

Natural immunity is slightly lower in normal pregnancy and pregnant women are rather more susceptible to most types of infection. The reason for the lowering of immunity is probably to allow the baby to grow and develop within the mother's body, so that the mother's body will not try to reject it. It is often difficult to recognize infection with listeria because the symptoms are usually very mild. They are frequently described as being like a very mild dose of flu with a slightly raised temperature and a general aching.

The reason why listeriosis (being infected with listeria) causes a more severe problem during pregnancy is because the bacteria can cross the placenta to infect the baby. The result for the baby varies with the stage of pregnancy at which the infection takes place. If the infection occurs in early pregnancy miscarriage may happen. In the middle of pregnancy it may cause premature labour, which may result in the birth of a stillborn baby. In later pregnancy the result may be that the baby develops the symptoms of listeriosis soon after birth, which can be very serious.

This may seem very frightening but it has to be put into context. Listeriosis is *very rare*; it affects only about one pregnancy in every 20,000 and if you follow the advice about avoiding foods with a high risk of causing listeria it is very unlikely that you will be affected. If it is suspected that a pregnant woman has caught listeriosis, blood tests can be taken to confirm the diagnosis. The treatment consists of taking antibiotics.

Listeria is an unusual bacterium because it can grow at the temperature of a typical fridge, i.e. around 4–5°C. The main food sources that are associated with listeria infection are certain types of cheese, pâté and ready-prepared cook-chill foods. Listed below are details of the foods which should be avoided.

CHEESE

There are only a few types which should not be eaten. Cheese is an important source of protein and calcium so avoid only those listed here.

Cheese to avoid whilst pregnant
Ripened soft cheeses, e.g. Brie, Camembert.
Blue-veined cheeses, e.g. Blue Brie, Cambozola, Danish Blue,
   Dolcelatte, Roquefort, Shropshire, Stilton, Stilton spread
   cheese
(These cheeses should be avoided whether they are unpasteurized
   or pasteurized.)
Feta cheese: the UK Department has not advised pregnant
   women to avoid this cheese but recently the US Government
   has advised that feta should be avoided.

Cheeses which are safe to eat whilst pregnant
Hard cheeses, e.g. Austrian smoked, Babybel, Caerphilly, Ched-
   dar, Cheshire, Derby, Edam, Gloucester, Gouda, Gruyère,
   Lancashire, Leicester, Parmesan, Wensleydale
Soft, cream and processed cheese, e.g. cottage and spread cheese,
   processed cheese, Philadelphia, Mozzarella

PÂTÉ

All types of pâtés, whether they are made from meat, vegetables
or fish, should be avoided unless they are canned or shrink-
wrapped and marked 'pasteurized'. Don't forget that a lot of pâtés
are made from liver, which should be avoided during pregnancy,
because of the high Vitamin A content (see page 103).

COOK-CHILL FOODS

Cook-chill foods are ready-prepared dishes or foods which are
sold chilled, for the customer to re-heat at home. It is important
to follow the manufacturer's instructions and reheat these foods
thoroughly until they are piping hot all the way through. They
can be reheated using a microwave or conventional oven. Only
buy cook-chill foods that are packaged and within their use-by
date.

   Some cook-chill foods can be eaten hot or cold, for example
ready-cooked chicken. You should always avoid eating these
products cold. Either reheat them thoroughly or avoid them

altogether. Always check that the use-by date has not expired before eating them.

Toxoplasmosis

Toxoplasmosis is an illness caused by a parasite called toxoplasma gondii. It is not usually dangerous for a healthy adult or child. As with listeriosis, if a person's immunity is lowered, the infection is dangerous, and this group includes pregnant women. If a pregnant woman catches toxoplasmosis there is a risk that this may pass to her baby. Should this happen, the baby can develop severe symptoms, including excess fluid within the brain (hydrocephalus), brain damage (which can cause mental handicap and epilepsy), and eye damage (which can cause partial sight loss or even blindness). Many people catch toxoplasmosis as an adult or child and the infection, which is relatively harmless, is known as acquired toxoplasmosis. When caught by an unborn baby from its mother, it is called congenital toxoplasmosis and this is what is dangerous. Again, though, the risk of toxoplasmosis must be put into context. It is even rarer than listeriosis, with the reported incidence being one baby affected for every 50,000 babies born. By the age of thirty, three out of every ten people will already have had the infection, probably without realizing it. Once you have had toxoplasmosis, immunity is lifelong and you will not get it again whether you are pregnant or not. If toxoplasmosis infection is suspected in a pregnant woman a blood test will be taken to confirm the diagnosis. If the result is positive she will be treated with antibiotics, which reduces by three-quarters the risk of the infection passing to her unborn baby.

The parasite causing toxoplasmosis has been found in raw meat and cat droppings and there are therefore certain steps which can be taken to minimize the risk of infection in pregnancy.

i. *Avoid eating raw or undercooked meat*
    The toxoplasma parasite is killed by thorough cooking. Do not eat any raw or undercooked meat (including meat

usually eaten raw, such as Parma ham). Always wash your hands thoroughly after handling raw meat.

ii. *Always wash vegetables and salads before eating them*
Cats sometimes have the toxoplasma parasite in their droppings, which can then pass into the soil. Vegetables and salads may be coated with the soil that they have grown in and thus be contaminated by the parasite. Always wash vegetables and salads thoroughly (including pre-washed salads) to remove any traces of soil.

iii. *Always wear gloves when gardening*
This is to prevent contamination, which may be present in garden soil after it has been fouled by cats, from being passed from your hands to your mouth. Wash your hands after gardening even if you have worn gloves.

GOAT'S MILK

Goat's milk sometimes contains toxoplasmosis so you should not drink it unless it has been pasteurized, sterilized or UHT (ultra-heat treated).

CONTACT WITH CATS AND KITTENS

While you are pregnant always wash your hands after handling cats and kittens. Avoid contact with stray cats and kittens.

Cat litter trays Where possible get somebody else to change the soiled litter and clean out the tray. If this isn't possible and you have to clean it out yourself, always wear rubber gloves when doing so. Wash the gloves afterwards and always wash your hands as well.

Salmonellosis

The salmonella bacterium is one of the commonest causes of food poisoning and its incidence is rising year by year in the UK. Some experts feel that this rise is because more doctors are notifying the Government about cases that they come across, whereas others feel that the rise reflects a genuine increase. Salmonella is different to the listeria and toxoplasmosis bugs because it affects only the mother and does not pass across to the baby. However, salmonella infection can cause a very severe and debilitating illness and the developing baby can be harmed by high temperatures in the mother. The main symptoms are severe vomiting and diarrhoea. There are about 200 different varieties of salmonella and the severity of the effects usually depends on the particular strain causing the infection. Some foods are a high risk for salmonella and these are:

EGGS

You should not eat raw eggs or foods with uncooked egg in them. You should eat only eggs which are cooked until both the white and yolk are solid. If a recipe, for example chocolate mousse, requires raw or partially cooked eggs, use pasteurized dried or liquid egg.

MAYONNAISE

All shop-bought mayonnaise and salad creams contain pasteurized egg and are therefore safe – homemade varieties should be avoided unless you know they contain pasteurized egg.

POULTRY AND RAW MEAT

Raw poultry and meat may be contaminated with salmonella or other food-borne bacteria. These bacteria are destroyed by cooking thoroughly at high temperatures. Always cook meat and especially poultry thoroughly before eating them to make sure any bacteria are destroyed.

However, the raw meat can contaminate other foods and kitchen equipment, so special care should be taken when handling it, in particular do not let raw meat and poultry or their juices come into contact with cooked food. Store raw and cooked food in separate parts of your fridge, with the raw food on the lower shelves.

ICE CREAM

Avoid the soft whip type ice cream from ice cream machines, particularly if bought from ice cream vans.

Other food-borne infections

Bacteria are all around us and have many beneficial functions apart from causing food spoilage. However, to minimize the chance of your becoming infected by *harmful* bacteria from food follow the simple rules listed below.

- Follow the advice on the previous pages about listeria, toxoplasmosis and salmonella.
- Milk-borne infections. Do not drink unpasteurized milk whether from cows, sheep or goats unless you have boiled the milk for at least two minutes beforehand.
- Unwrapped food bought from a delicatessen. Any prepared food that is not individually packaged and stamped with a use-by date and does not require further cooking at home is a high risk food for food poisoning. This includes cooked meats, for example ham and corned beef; cooked meat products, for example sausage rolls and Cornish pasties; and

prepared salads, for example coleslaw and potato salad. The reason for the increased risk with these foods is that if staff in a store do not scrupulously follow the correct food handling guidelines then the stock may not be rotated properly or their hands might not be clean (especially if they also handle money) and the food may be exposed to airborne bacteria. It must be emphasized that it is not because the above *foods* are at risk that pregnant women are advised to avoid them, but because the environment in which they are stored could be contaminated.

- Food that is preserved by smoking, salting and curing rather than cooking. Examples of this type of food are smoked salmon or smoked mackerel, cured meats, for instance Parma ham or *jambon cru*, and soused or pickled herrings. The curing process usually kills any harmful bacteria that might cause food poisoning, but because the food is not cooked again at home, as a precaution, it is recommended that pregnant women avoid it.
- Shellfish, for example prawns, cockles, mussels and whelks, are a major source of food poisoning and unless you buy them packaged and stamped with a use-by date or eat them in a restaurant or café which you know has a very good reputation, it is advisable for pregnant women to avoid these foods.

Water-borne infections

Water is a major vector or carrier of harmful bacteria. The UK, like many other countries, has effective water treatment policies and it is safe to drink tap water. Other countries do not have such policies, however, and the tap water is not safe. In these circumstances only boiled or bottled water should be drunk and used for washing fruit and vegetables and for making ice cubes. If you are not sure about the water source always be cautious until you are positive the tap water is safe to use.

GENERAL FOOD HANDLING GUIDELINES

- Keep your kitchen clean and dry – wash and dry utensils with a clean cloth between preparation stages. Always wash your hands with warm soapy water before preparing food.
- Take chilled and frozen foods home as quickly as possible and put them in the fridge or freezer immediately.
- Keep your fridge and freezer at the correct temperature. Fridges should be below 5°C. Freezers should be below −18°C. Fridge and freezer thermometers are inexpensive ways of monitoring the temperature.
- Cover foods in the fridge, and store raw and cooked foods separately; raw foods in the bottom of the fridge, and cooked foods at the top.
- Make sure frozen meats and fish are thoroughly defrosted before cooking, unless the directions on the pack specify otherwise. Defrost foods in a cool place, preferably in the fridge. Do not thaw them in a warm room.
- Check dates on goods, and use food within the recommended period.
- Cook food thoroughly until it is piping hot right through, particularly poultry and chilled or frozen prepared meals.
- Observe microwave standing times, stir microwaved food and check the food is piping hot in the middle.
- If you intend to reheat the food, ensure you chill it thoroughly after the first serving, and make sure it is piping hot before serving it again. Do not reheat food more than once.
- Do not eat raw eggs or foods containing raw eggs, such as homemade mayonnaise and homemade ice creams, mousses and cheesecakes.

ANIMAL-RELATED INFECTIONS THAT ARE POTENTIALLY HARMFUL FOR PREGNANT WOMEN

Infections from sheep

Sheep are potential carriers of some infections which are dangerous for pregnant women to catch. These are listeriosis and toxoplasmosis (described on pages 104 to 108) and a bacteria infection called chlamydia, which can be a rare cause of miscarriage. Pregnant women should not help with lambing, or milk ewes that have recently given birth, or touch the afterbirth (placenta) or come into contact with newborn lambs.

Infections from cats

Follow the advice about avoiding toxoplasmosis given on page 108.

Bovine Spongiform Encephalitis (BSE)

This is a very severe illness affecting cattle that is thought to be caused by feeding sheep brains to cattle. Since 1989 MAFF (Ministry of Agriculture, Fisheries and Food) has banned these feeding practices so one would expect the incidence of BSE to be falling in younger cattle. However, the incidence is *not* falling as fast as expected and there is no explanation for this, although one theory is that the disease is transmitted from cow to calf.

For a long time before BSE became so prevalent, sheep were infected with a similar disease called scrapie. If cattle become infected by eating scrapie-infected sheep products, there is a theoretical risk that other animal species, including man, could be infected by eating BSE-infected cattle.

Although there is no proven risk there may be cause for concern and some countries have banned the import of British

113

beef. Until there is more evidence, however, judgement cannot be made about the safety of eating British beef and beef products.

FOOD CONTAMINANTS

Food is sometimes (though inadvertently) contaminated by harmful substances such as heavy metals and residues left by the chemicals used in pesticides, herbicides and fungicides.

Heavy metal contamination

Mercury, lead, cadmium and nickel are all capable of causing handicaps in unborn babies. Mercury and nickel poisoning are almost unheard of in the UK. Cadmium is released with cigarette smoke and, as stated before, pregnant women are very strongly advised not to smoke or breathe in other people's smoke.

Exposure to lead in the UK usually comes either from water supplied by lead pipes or from breathing in relatively large amounts of car exhaust fumes. To reduce the risk of absorbing lead from water pipes if you know your house is supplied by lead piping, always let the tap run, especially first thing in the morning, before using the water for food or drink preparation. This will run off the water that has been stored in the pipes for a while. In some circumstances local water authorities will change the water pipes from lead to copper.

Pesticide residue contamination

Pesticides are designed not to leave harmful residues if they are to be used on food for human consumption. Occasionally problems do occur, but *very rarely* in Britain.

However, other pesticides, herbicides and fungicides are commonly used for a multitude of other purposes, for example as wood preservatives, paints and treatments, and for garden and household uses. Always follow the manufacturer's instructions exactly about correct ventilation and drying times. In some cases it may be sensible to avoid using these chemicals in early pregnancy. If you are not sure about a product's safety, check with the manufacturer first.

FOOD ADDITIVES

The UK's food manufacturers can legally choose from a list of about 300 food additives and 3,000 flavourings to add to the food they produce. Additives are used to improve the appearance, colour, keeping or safety qualities and flavour of food. All additives are chemicals, and some of these chemicals would occur naturally in the food but may have been lost during processing.

Additives used in the UK go through long and detailed safety tests before they are approved for use and continue to be monitored afterwards. Additives that are also approved for use throughout the European Community are given an E number, so some food additives can be referred to by an E number or chemical name or both. Any additive allowed in the UK is considered safe for almost everyone, but some people may react badly to them, for example some children become hyperactive when they have certain food colourings, and some preservatives provoke asthma attacks or skin rashes. The list of 300 additives is composed of three types:

i)   Natural, such as red colouring derived from beetroot juice (E162)
ii) Manmade 'twins' of something found in nature
iii) Manmade and not found in nature

If a food contains additives, they must be listed under the ingredients (however, only packaged foods will have a list of ingredients on them). The additive may be described by its E number or chemical name or both.

Additives fall into a number of categories:

Colours – E numbers E100–E199

Colours are added to foods to make them brighter and restore colour lost in processing. It is the yellow/orange ones (particularly E102 or tartrazine) that have been implicated in causing hyperactivity in children and there are strict limits about the addition of colourings to baby foods but not, unfortunately, to foods usually eaten by children, such as sweets, drinks, crisps.

Preservatives – E numbers E200–E299

Preservatives help to keep food safe for longer and protect against bacteria and fungi which cause food spoilage and food poisoning. They are safe for most people but this group does contain additives derived from benzoates and sulphates which have been implicated in asthma and skin rashes (known as urticaria).

Antioxidants – E numbers E300–E399

These are used in foods containing fat. When fat is exposed to the air (or oxygen) a reaction takes place and the fat becomes rancid. Rancid fats don't just taste bitter, they also pose a health risk. Antioxidants are added to stop oils and fats and fat-soluble vitamins (i.e. Vitamins A, D, E and K) from oxidizing and becoming rancid. Concern has been expressed about two antioxidants in particular, BHA (E320 or butylated hydroxyanisole) and BHT (E321 or butylated hydroxytolvene), but at the moment these are still permitted.

Emulsifiers and stabilizers – E numbers E400–E495

Emulsifiers and stabilizers are added to foods to ensure that they keep their shape and texture or are used to thicken foods. There is no concern about any of these being harmful to pregnant women.

Other miscellaneous additives – E numbers E500 upwards

There are a variety of reasons for adding these to foods – as glazing agents for confectionery, as anti-foaming agents to prevent frothing during processing, as propellant gases, for example in aerosol creams, or as flavour modifiers. Again, there is no concern at the moment about them being harmful to pregnant women.

ARTIFICIAL SWEETENERS

A few years ago the public became very concerned about the safety of artificial sweeteners, particularly cyclamates and saccharin, because of a link that was shown between their intake and cancer. However, the experiments were performed on mice, and the equivalent for humans of the amount that they were given is enormous even though sweeteners are added to foods in very tiny amounts.

Another theoretical risk was put forward about the sweetener aspartame (nutrasweet) because of the risk to women who did not know that they were carriers for a very rare disease called phenylketonuria.

All the sweeteners used in food and drink in the United Kingdom have undergone strenuous testing and pose no risk for anyone, including pregnant women.

HERBAL REMEDIES

Herbal remedies – commonly taken in the form of infusions (teas) and syrups – have been used by women for centuries in the belief that they would increase fertility, prevent miscarriage and alleviate labour pain and are still used in many parts of the world today, particularly China. Although there have been very few scientific assessments of herbal medicines for pregnancy there are many personal accounts of their beneficial properties.

However, before taking any preparations herbal or otherwise it is important to check that they are safe to take during pregnancy because there are many that are not (see below).

Herbs to avoid during pregnancy

The following herbs should be avoided during all stages of pregnancy because they can cause the uterus to contract. Check that any combined herbal preparations do not contain them.

arbor vitae	feverfew	nutmeg (*in large quantities*)
autumn crocus	golden seal	
barberry	greater celandine	pennyroyal
black cohosh	juniper	poke root
blood root	life root	rue
blue cohosh	male fern	southernwood
broom	mistletoe	tansy
cotton root	mugwort	thuja
		wormwood

Some herbs are recommended for easier labour, for example raspberry leaf tea, because they help you relax. However, they should never be taken before labour begins, and only then if it is the appropriate time for labour. This should be discussed in advance with your midwife.

Essential oils to avoid during pregnancy

The following essential oils (commonly used in aromatherapy or in the bath) should also be avoided during pregnancy.

basil	marjoram	pennyroyal
cinnamon bark	myrrh	savory
hyssop	nutmeg	thyme
juniper	oregano	

CHAPTER SIX

Common Pregnancy Problems

Pregnancy affects women in different ways. Some feel great throughout, others are not so lucky and suffer from a variety of complaints which, in some cases, if left untreated, could harm them and/or the baby. The symptoms that you experience are individual to your pregnancy and you cannot assume that you will feel the same as you felt in previous pregnancies, never mind the same as your friends. Read the following chapter so that you can reassure yourself that the symptoms you are feeling are typical. If you are at all worried, go and see your doctor or midwife.

EXCESSIVE TIREDNESS

You may feel excessively tired and lacking in energy, usually before you have even missed a period and know that you are pregnant. All you want to do is lie down and sleep, particularly in the afternoon and early evening. The tiredness is nothing to worry about and although it is a typical symptom of early pregnancy nobody really knows why it happens except perhaps that it is nature's way of telling you to 'slow down a bit' during pregnancy. The tiredness usually lasts only for the first three months, but if it continues longer or if you feel it is more than you can cope with, see your doctor. It may be that you are anaemic (see page 131 for more advice about anaemia) and need some treatment. But don't assume that because you feel so lethargic your diet is deficient and rush out and buy some vitamin or iron tablets as a tonic. Remember, check with your doctor/ midwife before you take any medicines/supplements when you are pregnant or planning to be in the near future, even if somebody else has told you that they are safe or that they were given to them when they were pregnant.

PASSING URINE FREQUENTLY

Again this is a common symptom of early pregnancy and nothing to worry about, even if you seem to be going to the loo all day and night. Some 'old wives' tales' suggest that this is nature's way of getting you used to having a broken night's sleep before the baby arrives! (See page 25 for the real reason.) It has nothing to do with how much you are drinking, so don't cut down on your intake of fluids. However, a word of caution; urinary infections are more common when you are pregnant, so, if you have any pain or a burning sensation when passing urine consult your doctor/midwife to check that you do not have an underlying infection.

MORNING SICKNESS OR PREGNANCY SICKNESS

This usually happens in early pregnancy and describes the symptoms of feeling sick (pregnancy nausea) or actually being sick (pregnancy vomiting). Although usually referred to as morning sickness because it occurs more often in the mornings (particularly just after rising) it can happen at any time of the day or night or, if you are really unlucky, for most of the day and night!

You may start feeling sick even before you have your pregnancy confirmed. The symptoms are most common between weeks 6 to 9, are usually worst around weeks 9 and 10, then start to disappear around weeks 12 to 14. The severity of symptoms is very variable and can range from just vague discomfort with certain cooking smells or feeling a bit queasy in the morning, to severe cases resulting in continuous vomiting making it impossible for you to work or look after young children.

Nobody really knows why pregnancy sickness happens but a number of theories have been put forward to explain it:

- The raised hormone (or chemical messenger) levels in pregnancy, particularly oestrogen and hCG (human chorionic gonadotrophin), which are released by the placenta in relatively large amounts in early pregnancy, may be responsible.

- Pyridoxine, also known as Vitamin B6 (see Table 10 in Appendix 2 for dietary sources), has been studied extensively to see if there is a link between a pregnant woman's diet being deficient in it and pregnancy sickness. The research available does not allow us to reach a firm conclusion, but it appears that giving Vitamin B6 supplements does not reduce the severity of pregnancy sickness in those women who have only mild symptoms, but may be helpful for women who suffer a more severe or extended form. It is sensible to include foods high in Vitamin B6 preconceptually and during early pregnancy, if you are prone to nausea and vomiting.

- Psychological factors, such as worrying about the pregnancy and the effects and changes that the baby will have on a settled lifestyle, may be responsible for pregnancy sickness in some women. Although it is difficult to decide if psychological factors are the only cause of the sickness, discussing your fears and anxieties with a friend, partner or midwife may help. If you think that seeing a social worker would be beneficial, ask the midwife to refer you to one.

Many women worry that because they are feeling sick and not eating very much, or vomiting up even the food that they *have* managed to eat, then the baby will not be growing properly. Although it may be logical to think that this might happen, in fact your body has a store of the necessary nutrients for early pregnancy and research work into this shows that women who suffer pregnancy sickness have the same chance of having a healthy baby as women who don't have any pregnancy sickness symptoms. The better your diet before conception the more likely it is that your nutrient stores will be full. This is another reason for planning ahead for your pregnancy if you can.

Whatever you can manage to eat and drink during these few weeks should be as nutritious as possible, for example, a glass of milk or fruit juice instead of a canned drink, a banana or bowl of breakfast cereal instead of a chocolate bar.

Knowing that your symptoms will probably not last for more than a few weeks does not make it any easier whilst you are going through it and feeling awful. There are, however, some steps that you can take to reduce the symptoms and severity of pregnancy sickness.

i) Avoid being hungry

Hunger increases pregnancy sickness, which is one reason why it is thought to be so common when you get up in the morning after going without food overnight. The answer is to try to eat 'little and often', by not going more than two hours without having something to eat or drink during the day and evening. Also try eating something before getting up in the morning. Choose plain starchy foods such as bread, toast, chapati, plain biscuits, a banana or other fruit, a jacket potato, rice, pasta or a bowl of breakfast cereal. Other things worth trying are a carton of yoghurt or fromage frais. It may be that you can manage only very small portions of these foods but that does not matter. It would be ideal if the food and drink that you do manage to eat were the sort recommended for during pregnancy, but it is just as important to try to hold something down, so anything which fits this bill would be acceptable in the short term.

ii) Avoid strong-smelling food and drink and other everyday odours

There are certain food smells that seem to trigger pregnancy sickness more than others. This is particularly so if the food is hot, or fried, or spicy. Ask your partner or a friend or relative to do the cooking for a while (though this is not much help if your job includes cooking, in which case see if it is possible to have a temporary change of duties). Alternatively, try eating just cold food for a while. This is not as odd as it sounds, and cold food is often more nutritious than hot food because of the vitamin losses that can occur during cooking.

Tea and coffee are frequently cited by women in early pregnancy as having an unpleasant smell (and taste) and are often a trigger for pregnancy sickness. Switch to alternative drinks such as milk or fruit juice or water.

There are a wide range of other smells that may trigger pregnancy sickness, but the most common ones are petrol, tobacco, tar and perfume. The obvious answer is to try to avoid whatever upsets you.

iii) Avoid long journeys, especially in the back of cars

Whether or not you normally suffer from travel sickness you may find that whilst you are pregnant you do experience it, or it is more severe than when you were not pregnant. One reason for this could be that many working women travel in the mornings and evenings when they may also be hungry because they did not feel like eating in the morning or during the working day. Try travelling in the front of the car and avoid reading or looking down. Ensure that the car is well ventilated unless you are in a traffic jam, when the fumes can make things worse.

Don't forget that short-term pregnancy sickness is very common – about seven out of every ten women suffer from it – and it does not in any way mean that you are not going to have a healthy, successful pregnancy. Read the guidelines in Chapter 2 about weight gain in early pregnancy if you are worried that you are losing weight because of the sickness.

Occasionally, pregnancy sickness is very severe (affecting 3.5 per 1000 pregnant women), causing constant and uncontrolled vomiting so that it is impossible even to keep water down. This can lead to your body being short of fluid and salt (dehydrated) and a rapid weight loss. This condition is known as Severe Pregnancy Vomiting (or hyperemesis gravidarum) and usually requires medical treatment, which may result in a short hospital stay. The treatment consists of correcting the dehydration by restoring fluid and salt, and sometimes the only way to do this is via a glucose or saline drip in the arm. Drinks are then introduced, usually starting with sips of water and gradually building up to first larger amounts and then other drinks such as fruit juice, lemonade or milk. Sometimes, if there has been large weight and other nutrient loss, the drip can also be used to deliver full feeding in liquidized form.

During this time a woman will need a great deal of support and reassurance that she can continue to have a healthy and successful pregnancy. As soon as possible when she can face food again small amounts that will tempt her appetite are given. This can be a problem with hospital food, in which case relatives who will probably have a better understanding of the individual's food likes and dislikes may be asked to supplement the hospital diet. As with a typical case of pregnancy sickness, fried and spicy dishes are often not well tolerated and it is a good idea not to take drinks with food but to have them in between.

As with milder pregnancy sickness, the precise cause of severe pregnancy vomiting is not known, although the same factors are thought to be implicated. Psychological factors may be particularly relevant if a woman had a strong fear of changes to her body image and/or a history of eating disorders such as anorexia nervosa or bulimia.

One reassuring thought, though, is that hyperemesis gravidarum happens much more frequently in women having their first babies so if you go through it once it is much less likely that you will suffer it again in later pregnancies.

CRAVINGS AND AVERSIONS

Liking or disliking food and drink (or even the smell of them) in a way that is different to how you felt before pregnancy is known as experiencing dietary cravings and aversions. A food or drink that you suddenly like is a craving and a food that you have competely gone off is an aversion. These are very common in early pregnancy and although the precise mechanism causing them is not known there are probably physical and psychological factors involved. Evidence for a physical cause is that raised pregnancy hormones, particularly oestrogen, may be responsible, through effects on the brain. This theory is supported by some research carried out on women who in later life developed brain tumours and experienced dietary cravings and aversions similar to those that they had many years ago when pregnant.

The reason why cravings and aversions are thought to have a possible psychological origin is that the cravings and aversions arise subconsciously in a pregnant woman who is trying to improve her diet and avoid food and drink that she perceives to be unhealthy. This theory holds as long as the dietary changes are based on the sound nutrition principles discussed in Chapter 4 and not on inaccurate old wives' tales – ideas such as that sour foods like lemon juice and vinegar will make the baby sour (or bad) tempered, taking cod liver oil will make the baby slip out easily, eating strawberries will cause the baby to have a birth mark, or drinking a pint of milk a day will ensure an adequate supply of breast milk! Many of the old wives' tales are harmless, but some, for instance taking cod liver oil in early pregnancy (see page 18) or certain herbal remedies (see page 118), may be harmful, so discuss them first with your doctor/midwife.

As a general rule, as long as the dietary cravings and aversions you experience do not stop you following a sensible eating pattern most of the time, go ahead and don't worry if you need pickled onions with your ice cream! Different ethnic cultures have their own folklore about food and pregnancy which again may be totally harmless or potentially dangerous and you should always check out the theories with your doctor/midwife.

The most common food aversions are for tea, coffee and meat, especially pork and liver (in fact liver should always be avoided during pregnancy, see page 103). The most common food cravings are for sweets and chocolate, milk and dairy foods, fruit and fruit juice and very cold food like ice cream. A craving for sweets and chocolate may be acceptable if it doesn't last too long!

PICA

Pica is the name given to a rare form of dietary craving which involves the compulsive desire to eat non-food items, for example coal, clay, starch, mothballs, toothpaste, soil, baking soda, soot, charcoal and chalk. Pica is very rare and not limited to any particular group of women. Many theories have been put forward to explain pica but none of them are very convincing and it is still not known why it happens. One theory is that without knowing it herself, i.e. subconsciously, a pregnant woman believes that she is lacking in certain nutrients and is trying to correct the deficiency by eating substances that contain the nutrient. This could apply to eating chalk to obtain calcium, but unfortunately it won't work because calcium is not absorbed in that form. Pica can lead to dietary deficiencies because some of the substances eaten reduce absorption of minerals such as iron. Pica may also result in poisoning and infection. If you have a craving for a non-food item, consult your midwife.

HEARTBURN

Heartburn is not related to heart problems but describes the burning sensation in the middle of the chest caused by stomach acid escaping back up your food pipe or oesophagus and irritating it. Your stomach is lined with a sticky mucus to stop the acid irritating it but your food pipe is not, hence the burning sensation. Heartburn is not a problem for some pregnant women, but in others it makes them feel very uncomfortable. It is more common after eating and usually worse in the later stages of pregnancy when the abdomen is filled by the pregnant womb. There are certain steps that you can take to alleviate the symptoms of heartburn but if they still persist ask your doctor for an antacid medicine that is safe for you to take while you are pregnant.

- Eat slowly and chew your food thoroughly.

- Eat smaller, more frequent meals rather than larger, well spaced ones.
- Sit up straight when eating and don't lie down for the first hour after eating.
- Try to be relaxed when eating.
- Avoid foods that may upset the stomach, such as spicy food.
- Don't eat very hot or very cold foods.
- Don't drink with meals, but wait until half an hour afterwards.
- Avoid fizzy drinks which may induce you to bring up wind, which may cause the acid in your stomach to come up into the oesophagus.
- Sleep propped up by extra pillows to avoid heartburn during the night.
- Milk helps to neutralize the acid in your stomach whether it is skimmed, semi-skimmed, full fat or soya, so drink these in preference to other drinks.
- Don't wear tight clothes around your abdomen.

CONSTIPATION

Constipation is the name given to the condition when the bowel movements are either reduced or the stools are hard and difficult to pass. You should remember that everyone is individual in their bowel habits and what is normal for one person may not be appropriate for another. Constipation can cause discomfort, often with a bloated feeling or cramps in the abdomen. Constipation is more common in pregnancy because the pregnancy hormones tend to relax the intestinal muscles and make them sluggish. The pressure of the growing baby on the lower part of the bowel may also make passing stools more difficult than usual, particularly in the later part of pregnancy.

The following advice may help to reduce the incidence and symptoms of constipation.

- Drink plenty of water each day – six to eight glasses per day on top of your usual drinks of juice, tea, coffee, etc.
- Follow a diet high in fibre (sometimes called roughage). Good sources of fibre are listed in Table 3, Appendix 2. Insoluble dietary fibre is found only in plant foods, is not digested and bulks up the stools in the intestine making them easier to pass. If you are not used to taking much fibre, start increasing the intake slowly and gradually build up. A sudden increase of fibre intake may lead to bloating and flatulence.
- Iron tablets prescribed for anaemia sometimes cause constipation – if you think that this is the case for you, discuss the problem with your midwife because not all iron supplements have this effect and it should be possible to find an alternative. The side effects of any iron supplements will be reduced if the tablets are taken about one hour before meals.

Sometimes following the dietary advice does not work, particularly if you suffered from constipation before pregnancy, and a mild laxative may be prescribed. The type to use are those containing bulking agents which will make your stools larger and softer and therefore easier to pass. There are many different brands of these laxatives that are safe to take during pregnancy so ask your midwife to suggest a suitable one.

HAEMORRHOIDS

These are also often known as 'piles' and although they don't just happen during pregnancy they are more common then. They are caused by enlarged veins in the lower bowel which can sometimes bulge through the anus. These enlarged veins are made worse by the weight of the baby pressing down on the lower bowel and, if you are constipated, by straining to pass stools. They may be painful, uncomfortable and itchy and they can bleed.

Steps to avoid haemorrhoids:

- Rest if possible during the afternoon to reduce the pressure of the baby pressing down on the bowel when you are standing.
- Avoid constipation by following the high-fibre dietary advice on the previous page which will help you to produce soft, easy-to-pass stools.
- Always wash the anal area after passing a stool as this helps to alleviate itching.
- If the haemorrhoids are causing you a lot of discomfort, ask your midwife to suggest a suitable soothing cream which will ease the problem.

FEELING FULL

This is usually a greater problem towards the end of your pregnancy and especially if you are expecting more than one baby. It is caused by the growing womb exerting pressure on the stomach. When you eat, the stomach cannot expand as much as usual, hence there is a full feeling before the meal is finished. The remedy lies in having small, frequent meals and snacks rather than three larger meals a day. Do not drink with these small meals/snacks but wait until about half an hour afterwards.

THRUSH (CANDIDA)

If you are prone to thrush infections in the vagina, they may be more of a problem than usual during pregnancy. Itching or discharge from the vulva are the usual symptoms. A simple pessary from your doctor will usually clear the infection.

ANAEMIA

Anaemia is a blood disorder caused by a lack of various components needed to make your blood healthy. The lack of these components, resulting in anaemia in pregnancy, is nearly always caused by a lack of certain nutrients in the diet. An individual may need more of these nutrients, especially iron, folic acid and Vitamin B12, during pregnancy and if dietary intake is not adequate, anaemia is the result.

Iron deficiency anaemia

During pregnancy you need to eat plenty of iron-rich foods so that you can manufacture new red blood cells and those of your baby. Your baby needs more iron during the last three months of pregnancy so that when it is born it has adequate iron stores and won't become anaemic in early infancy. The baby draws iron from the mother for its own requirements so the mother may develop iron deficiency anaemia but the baby probably won't. (Women with iron deficiency anaemia tend to have lower birthweight babies whether they are born premature or at 40 weeks [term].)

CAUSES OF IRON DEFICIENCY ANAEMIA IN PREGNANCY

- Low iron stores before pregnancy – when planning a pregnancy ensure that you eat adequate amounts of iron-rich foods (see Table 17, Appendix 2), particularly if you previously suffered from heavy periods.
- Previous regular use of aspirin. This can cause the loss of repeated small amounts of blood from the stomach.
- Previous blood donation of more than three times a year.
- Twins or triplets.
- Having a baby less than one year after a previous one.
- Not having an adequate dietary intake of Vitamin C (see Table 13 in Appendix 2 for good sources of Vitamin C).

- Having an inadequate vegetarian diet, i.e. cutting meat out of the diet without adding back enough iron from other sources (see Table 17 in Appendix 2 for sources of iron in food).
- Teenage pregnancy.
- Low income, which may make an adequate diet difficult to obtain.
- Having had four or more children.

STEPS USED TO PREVENT OR TREAT IRON DEFICIENCY ANAEMIA

1. *Increasing the iron in your diet*
Good sources of iron are shown in Table 17 in Appendix 2.

2. *Increasing the amount of iron you absorb from your diet*
There are a number of steps you can take to maximize the absorption of iron from your diet – see page 72 for information on this.

3. *Iron tablets*
At one time all pregnant women were given iron tablets to take, but now they are usually prescribed only if your haemoglobin level is low or if your doctor thinks you have a high risk of developing anaemia. Some women experience side effects from iron tablets, including heartburn, nausea, abdominal discomfort, constipation and diarrhoea. These symptoms can be reduced by taking the iron tablets about one hour before meals. They should be taken with water or a drink high in Vitamin C, for example orange juice, not tea or coffee, to increase their effectiveness. Iron tablets should be taken only if they have been prescribed by a doctor.

Folic acid deficiency anaemia

Folic acid is a general term used to describe a group of compounds similar to folic acid, a B vitamin. It is a vitamin that your body does not store for a long time and therefore you need a regular supply. Folic acid is perhaps the most important vitamin for pregnancy because of its role in preventing neural tube defects such as spina bifida in early pregnancy and its function in cell division in body tissues.

If you become deficient in folate in later pregnancy you might develop a type of anaemia.

Vitamin B12 deficiency anaemia

Vitamin B12 or cobalamin, like folate, is also important for forming red blood cells and so deficiency of it can lead to anaemia.

LEG CRAMPS

Many women suffer painful leg cramps when pregnant, particularly at night. Many things have been put forward to explain this, including a lack of dietary calcium and phosphorus or an excessive intake of caffeine from tea and coffee and cola-type drinks. None of these theories has been scientifically proven, and no treatment has been shown to work.

PRE-ECLAMPSIA OR PREGNANCY-INDUCED HYPERTENSION

Pre-eclampsia is the most common serious complication of pregnancy affecting one out of every ten women. The symptoms of pre-eclampsia (also known as pregnancy-induced hypertension and toxaemia) are high blood pressure, excessive fluid retention (known as oedema) and protein present in the urine. It usually occurs in women having their first baby and during the last half of pregnancy. Pre-eclampsia occurs more frequently in women whose placenta is abnormally large (for example diabetic women and those with multiple pregnancies), and also those with high blood pressure before pregnancy.

Family studies have indicated a genetic predisposition, with daughters of women who experienced pre-eclampsia having a higher incidence than daughters whose mothers were not affected by it.

Many women with pre-eclampsia do not have any symptoms, but some women experience headaches, visual disturbances and abdominal pains. Careful checks are made on pregnant women to try to detect the early signs of pre-eclampsia, including blood pressure measurements and urine testing so that evasive action can be taken before it develops into the much more serious condition eclampsia.

Interest in nutritional causes of pre-eclampsia arose for three reasons. First, it was thought to be more common in areas where vegetarianism was prevalent (i.e. the population was largely non-meat-eating, with possibly a low protein diet) and there were differences in the incidence of it between developed and developing countries. These reports have since been found to be inaccurate.

Second, dietary deficiencies were thought to be the cause of pre-eclampsia because the incidence fell during the Second World War (1939–45) and increased afterwards. However, the fall in pre-eclampsia in the early part of the war preceded the food shortage and began to rise before the food supply was increased after the war, so dietary restrictions were not the cause. However, dietary supplements could have helped. A large-scale study carried out during the war by the People's League of Health gave one group of women a supplement containing, amongst other nutrients, halibut liver oil, calcium and the antioxidant vitamins A and C. Page 138 describes in greater detail the evidence that leads to the conclusion that a lack of these particular nutrients may cause pre-eclampsia.

At the end of the Second World War in Holland food was very scarce, with only about 600 calories per person per day at its worst being available, and this was associated with a decrease in pre-eclampsia. However, the famine resulted in far fewer babies being conceived and many being born premature, which, because pre-eclampsia usually occurs in the latter part of pregnancy, would also reduce the incidence.

Third, there was thought to be an association of pre-eclampsia with social class, since it was more common among poor women who, it was assumed, also had a poor diet. Other factors such as lack of sanitation, not having a free health service and thus access to antenatal care were not taken into account.

At the moment the cause of pre-eclampsia is unknown but there is still a great deal of scientific interest in nutritional causes. It seems likely that certain dietary factors may influence the triggers for pre-eclampsia without being the direct cause and the following paragraphs give further details.

Excessive maternal weight and weight gain

Women who are overweight are more likely to develop high blood pressure during pregnancy and possibly pre-eclampsia. Women who are very underweight before pregnancy also have a slightly higher risk of developing pre-eclampsia. This is another reason why being the appropriate weight for your height before pregnancy is so important (see Chapter 1).

Gaining large amounts of weight in the second half of pregnancy is associated with a slightly increased risk of pre-eclampsia but it is explained in part by an excess accumulation of body fluid.

Many obstetricians, particularly in the United States, tried to prevent pre-eclampsia by advising women to restrict their weight gain. However, in order to restrict weight gain a wide variety of dietary advice was given – women were told to follow low carbohydrate diets, low fat diets, high protein diets and low calorie diets – so isolating the particular dietary factor responsible was impossible. Also, giving such strict dietary advice made it necessary for the women to attend antenatal clinics more often, making it more likely that the early symptoms of pre-eclampsia were picked up and treatment given. So the claim that low weight gain affected the incidence of pre-eclampsia is not strictly true.

Protein

Pre-eclampsia is often accompanied by low levels of protein in the mother's blood and as early as the second half of the seventeenth century doctors were advising women to increase their dietary protein intake. A decrease in the incidence of pre-eclampsia in Germany during the First World War was attributed to a lack of meat (a major source of protein) in the diet. The low protein theory was taken seriously for a long time and is still advocated by Thomas Brewer.

The Brewer Diet

Thomas Brewer, an American obstetrician, has made a study of the dietary treatment to prevent pre-eclampsia, and since the publication of his book *Metabolic Toxaemia of Late Pregnancy: a Disease of Malnutrition*, a charity called The Pre-Eclamptic Toxaemia Society, advocating his principles, has been established in the UK (PETS). They advocate a high-protein, low-carbohydrate, diet and claim that:

'Medical research has shown that poor diets during the course of pregnancy may cause:

1 Stillborn babies
2 Low birthweight or premature babies
3 Brain-damaged babies with low intelligence
4 Hyperactive irritable babies
5 Babies more susceptible to illness
6 Pre-eclampsia, eclampsia (epileptic fits caused by high blood pressure in pregnancy)
7 Anaemia in the mother
8 Severe infections of the lungs, kidneys and liver in the mother
9 Placental separation leading to bleeding before the birth
10 Miscarriage'

These claims have not been thoroughly tested and two scientific studies performed in Motherwell, Scotland, and in New York, USA, have shown that providing pregnant women with high protein diets or supplements will result in a decrease in the birthweight of the baby which is potentially very harmful (see page 57).

Our conclusion is that the evidence that a lack of dietary protein causes pre-eclampsia is not based on scientific fact, but the evidence that a very high dietary protein intake during pregnancy is harmful is conclusive.

Salt

Excess dietary salt has been linked with high blood pressure in both men and women, so it seems logical to link dietary salt and pre-eclampsia. Salt restriction was practised widely on pregnant pre-eclamptic women for the treatment of oedema (excess body fluid retention). Two research studies comparing high and low salt diets failed to show any differences, except in one of the studies; women on the high salt diet had a lower incidence of pre-eclampsia – the opposite of what was expected!

Calcium

In 1942, as already explained, a committee set up by the People's League of Health tried to improve the diet of British mothers by giving them a supplement containing iron, calcium, iodine, manganese, copper, Vitamin B complex, Vitamin C and halibut liver oil. The incidence of pre-eclampsia was reduced.

Claims about the beneficial effects of calcium were made by various doctors based on this evidence but these claims were not substantiated until recently, when a study was carried out on women living in Ecuador who have a low dietary calcium intake. Pregnant women thought to be at risk of developing pre-eclampsia were divided into two groups – half were given calcium supplements and half were given a similar-looking tablet (or placebo) that did not contain calcium. Only 1 in 6 of the calcium-supplemental group developed pre-eclampsia but three-quarters of the placebo (no calcium) group did. This study will have to be repeated on larger groups of women to make sure the results are sound but they are certainly interesting. (To check that you are having enough calcium in your diet, see Table 14 in Appendix 2.)

Fish oils

Another component of the supplement given by the People's League of Health in 1942 was halibut liver oil. Halibut liver oil contains essential fatty acids which your body cannot make itself so you need a regular supply in your diet (see page 56 for further details). Essential fatty acids are present in large amounts in the human eyes and brain, and are important in producing the chemicals which affect blood pressure and blood clotting. Circumstantial support for the role of fish oils comes from the Faeroe Islands where women consume a diet rich in fish oil. The incidence of pre-eclampsia is lower than on the mainland but a direct link to essential fatty acid consumption has yet to be proved. A large research study is currently being performed to see if the addition of fish oil to the mother's diet reduces her risk of pre-eclampsia.

But be aware – some fish liver oils are very high in Vitamin A. Taking too much Vitamin A particularly in early pregnancy is unwise (see page 17 for further details).

Antioxidant vitamin supplements

The antioxidant or ACE vitamins, i.e. Vitamins A, C and E, help to prevent damage to body tissues. An interesting theory is that the supplement given to women during the Second World War by the People's League of Health reduced the incidence and severity of pre-eclampsia or PIH because it contained the antioxidant vitamins and some minerals.

URINE INFECTIONS

During pregnancy it is very common for sugar to be detected in the urine. This usually doesn't cause any problems, but bacteria thrive in sugary fluids and this can lead to the development of urinary infections. These should be treated with appropriate antibiotics prescribed by a doctor. A high fluid intake (8–10 cups per day) will flush the bladder and urinary tract through more quickly making it less likely that urinary infections will develop.

BACKACHE

Backache is very common in pregnancy and is caused by the softening and stretching of the pelvic ligaments. Again, there is no specific dietary treatment, but excess weight gain will aggravate the problem so follow the advice in Chapter 2 to gain the appropriate amount of weight. If the symptoms are severe consult your doctor.

THIRD DEGREE PERINEAL TEAR

During the delivery of a baby a third degree tear occasionally occurs – this is when the vagina is torn and the tear extends as far as the anal sphincter or rectum. Alternatively you may be cut (episiotomy) to ease the birth. Although this is not strictly a dietary matter, straining to pass stools can cause the wound to re-open. A high fibre diet (see dietary advice for constipation on page 000) and/or a commercial bulking agent such as Fybogel or Lactulose will add bulk to the stools. It is important to drink plenty of liquids.

CHAPTER SEVEN

After the Birth

BREASTFEEDING

We would always recommend breastfeeding, even if only for a short time, because of the benefits for the baby. Almost every woman can breastfeed successfully, and should be encouraged and helped to do so by both partners and relatives.

During breastfeeding it is important to continue the healthy eating and general lifestyle pattern established before or during the pregnancy. Coping with a new baby is tiring, so you need to look after yourself in order to do this. In addition, maintaining a healthy diet for yourself and your family is likely to have long-term health benefits for all of you.

The benefits of breastfeeding

Human milk is the natural food for human infants; it is therefore not surprising that a number of advantages associated with breastfeeding for both infants and mothers have been identified.

1 Breast milk is nutritionally superior to any alternative; the amount and type of each constituent is just right for your baby and its composition changes with your baby's changing needs as it grows. It is easily digested and is less likely to cause tummy upsets or diarrhoea.
2 Breast milk is safe, it is always fresh, and it contains a variety of anti-infectious factors and antibodies which pass resistance to certain infections on to your baby. There is a lot of evidence which suggests that breastfeeding reduces

the number of infant illnesses such as colds, coughs and chest infections, especially in the early months of life.

3 Breast milk is the least likely to cause allergic diseases (such as asthma and eczema) compared with any other infant food.

4 Breastfed babies are less likely to be overfed and the complications associated with improper dilutions of formula feeds are not concerns for breastfed babies.

5 Breastfeeding promotes good jaw and tooth development.

6 Breastfeeding automatically promotes close mother–child contact.

7 Early breastfeeding stimulates contractions of the uterus which helps the blood loss after childbirth to be completed more quickly.

8 Breastfeeding is generally more convenient once the process is established.

9 Breastfeeding is cheap.

10 Women who breastfeed for a year or more tend to lose weight more easily, especially around the thighs and buttocks.

11 Women who have breastfed are less likely to develop cancer of the breasts in later life.

Although breastfeeding is certainly the best way to feed a baby, it is not always easy, especially if you live in a society such as ours where it is hidden and women rarely get the chance to learn by observation how to do it as they grow up. Some women find breastfeeding easy right from the start, but many find it difficult to do without help. Do ask for assistance and advice from your trained carers – your midwives and health visitors. Also there are three national voluntary organizations which offer leaflets, information and advice on breastfeeding. They or your midwife or health visitor may also be able to put you in touch with a local support group or with a breastfeeding counsellor (see Useful Addresses, Appendix 3). An excellent book to prepare you is *Bestfeeding* by Mary Renfrew, Chloe Fisher and Suzanne Arms, published by Celestial Arts, Berkeley, California. It is a guide to getting breastfeeding right and solving problems quickly and easily. It contains many detailed photographs and illustrations that help you to see exactly what to do.

Breast milk can provide all the nourishment your baby needs for optimal growth for at least 4–6 months and for the following few months can continue to be a major source of nutrients while the transition to solid food is made. Some women continue to breastfeed for over two years because of the enjoyment it brings to themselves and their child. This pattern of feeding is not possible for all women, but remember that breastfeeding even for a short time is better for mother and baby than not breastfeeding at all.

The production of breast milk and its release

The pregnancy hormones prepare the breasts for breastfeeding and ensure the production of the early milk or colostrum. The volume of this early milk is small, as are the needs of the newborn baby. However, as soon as the baby is born, the milk-producing hormone, prolactin, acts within the breasts to encourage the production of a greater milk supply. In addition, the more your baby feeds, the greater is the amount of prolactin released by the brain and the more signals your breasts receive to produce milk. The milk is released from the breast by the 'letdown reflex'. This involves the small muscles around the areas where milk is stored in the breasts contracting and squeezing the milk out. The hormone responsible for triggering the letdown reflex is oxytocin, and when you feed your baby (or perhaps just think about feeding your baby) your brain will release oxytocin and your breasts will 'let down' the milk. In the first few days after the birth you may find that as you breastfeed you can feel your uterus contracting (rather painfully in some cases, especially if it's your second or third child). This is due to the action of oxytocin (it was this hormone which also produced your contractions in labour), which is helping you to clear your body of the blood it needs to lose and helping your uterus to contract down to size.

The composition of breast milk

The components of breast milk include protein, fat, sugar (lactose), minerals such as calcium and iron, vitamins and a large proportion of water. The amounts of these substances breast milk contains, however, is never constant. The milk produced during the first two or three days is different to the milk produced after this initial stage, which in turn is different to the milk produced after a few months. Milk composition also changes throughout every breastfeed and varies from woman to woman.

The first milk your body produces is called colostrum. It looks yellowish and creamy in comparison with the thinner and sometimes slightly bluish colour of mature milk which begins to flow after two or three days. Colostrum is higher in protein and minerals and lower in carbohydrates and fat than mature milk and it contains a greater amount of the protective antibodies which help to prevent infection by bacteria and viruses. It also helps babies to pass the thick, green/black meconium (the first stool). This is important in avoiding the development of jaundice.

Mature breast milk contains a relatively higher proportion of carbohydrate and fat, necessary for the rapid growth of your baby, and its composition changes in an important way throughout every breastfeed. The fore milk which your baby takes at first is high in volume and low in fat, and could be considered as a 'drink' at the start of every feed. As your baby feeds, the amount of milk she gets slows down too. Her sucking will slow down, with longer pauses between periods of sucking, and she will now be getting the hind milk which is higher in calories. This richer hind milk can be thought of as the 'food' part of the feed. It is essential that your baby gets a good balance of both the fore milk and the hind milk and it is best to let your baby be the judge of this, which you can do by following these guidelines:

- Let her feed whenever she seems hungry; this will probably be every two or three hours for the first few weeks.

- Let her stay on each breast until she has had enough and comes off herself, i.e. let your baby finish the first breast first, then offer her the second side. Sometimes she will have had enough with one.

The composition of your breast milk is also, to some extent, influenced by your diet and this will be discussed in the following section.

Your diet while breastfeeding

While you are breastfeeding your calorie requirements will be higher than during your pregnancy. Some of the energy required to make your breast milk is provided by the body fat you stored during pregnancy, however, the majority is provided by your daily food intake. Appetite during the first few weeks will be the best guide to how much to eat; recent studies have suggested that the increase in intake is in the region of 300–400 calories per day above the pre-pregnant intakes. Try to ensure that the extra foods you eat reflect a nutritious and balanced increase and are based on starchy carbohydrates and fruit and vegetables with a small increase in protein intake, rather than alleviating your hunger with foods high in fats and sugars, such as chocolate bars, cakes and biscuits. Refer to Chapter 4 for more specific information and advice on food choices.

If you do not increase the amount of food you eat, the quantity and quality of your milk will not be affected but you are likely to feel tired. If you severely restrict your food intake, the ability to make milk will be affected. This is especially so during the early weeks when breastfeeding is being established. It is also advisable to spread your intake evenly throughout the day rather than just having one large meal in the evening.

As well as your appetite increasing you are likely to feel more thirsty than usual, which is not surprising when you consider that the baby will be taking 600–800 mls (over a pint) of fluid from you each day. Often you will feel thirsty during a feed, so having a drink beside you when you feed may be helpful. Try to drink more water or fruit juice rather than tea or coffee as too much caffeine can affect the baby (see page 102). Drinking plenty of fluids during this time can help prevent constipation too. However, there is no need to force yourself to drink more – just drink as much as you want to.

Listed below are a few questions on diet commonly asked by breastfeeding women, together with our responses:

Do I need to continue to avoid any of the foods which were high risk during pregnancy?
No, you can resume your normal diet (but still follow the general good food hygiene notes on page 112). Your baby is no longer at risk now she is not in direct contact with your blood supply. Also you are at less risk of infection as your immune system, which was depressed during pregnancy, will be operating normally again.

Will I be able to breastfeed if I don't drink milk?
Yes, you will. You don't need to drink cow's milk to make human milk. Cows don't drink any other animal's milk! However, if you don't drink milk or use it in cooking, you need to ensure you are getting calcium from alternative sources such as cheese and yoghurt or, if you don't eat any dairy products, foods such as oily fish, some green leafy vegetables, almonds, Brazil nuts, hazelnuts, sunflower seeds and sesame seeds. (See Table 14 in Appendix 2 for a more extensive list.)

Are there any problems associated with following a vegetarian diet?
Providing you are following the basic principles of sensible vegetarian eating you should have no problems with maintaining adequate quality and quantity of your breast milk. If dairy products are not acceptable to you, extra energy, high quality protein and calcium should be obtained from appropriately combined vegetables, pulses, cereals and nuts (see pages 88 to 91). Vegans are also at risk of being short of Vitamin B12. Some vegetables and foods of vegetable origin contain small amounts of

this vitamin (yeast, soya beans, comfrey, wheatgerm and some fermented foods), but it would be advisable to seek advice from a dietitian as to whether you should take a supplement.

Are any vitamin or mineral supplements advisable whilst breastfeeding?
Vitamin and mineral supplements should not be necessary if you are following a well-balanced diet. Calcium supplementation may be necessary if you are avoiding dairy products and you are not able to alter your diet to obtain enough calcium from alternative sources. If your diet is deficient in calcium, mobilization of calcium from your bones to maintain milk calcium levels will occur. Likewise, with other minerals such as iron, your body stores will be used to maintain breast milk levels if your intake is low. The vitamin content of breast milk is more dependent on your intake, thus if your intake of a vitamin is consistently low, the level in your milk will also be low. If you are avoiding certain foods for any reason and you are worried that your diet may not be adequate, consult a dietitian for advice (your midwife or health visitor should be able to put you in touch with one).

Should I be cautious about my intake of food additives (preservatives, flavourings, colourings, artificial sweeteners, etc)?
There is no specific advice on using these substances whilst breastfeeding (see page 115). All E-numbered additives have been 'approved' by the EC; however, there are still controversies surrounding some additives. We would advise that a limited intake should be fine if you yourself do not have any adverse reactions, and that eating healthily, including plenty of fresh foods, should eliminate the need for too much reliance on highly processed foods.

If breast milk is supposed to be the perfect food for my baby, why have I been advised that he should (a) have an injection/oral dose of Vitamin K soon after birth, (b) take a fluoride supplement and (c) take vitamin drops?
(a) The current DOH advice is that all infants should receive Vitamin K supplementation at birth. This is because bleeding disorders in babies, which very occasionally cause death, have

been associated with Vitamin K deficiency. There is much debate about whether this 'blanket' supplementation is warranted considering the low rate of occurrence of the disease (27 cases in a survey of 1.7 million births) and also as to whether breast milk really is deficient in Vitamin K (the majority of affected babies were found to have been breastfed). Recent work which has found Vitamin K in higher concentrations in colostrum and in hind milk may perhaps be an important finding in the debate, since arbitrary rules for breastfeeding management (four-hourly feeds, ten minutes each side, etc.) which have been quoted until relatively recently may have prevented the higher concentration of Vitamin K from reaching the baby. There is also the controversy about the method of administration of Vitamin K; recent research has suggested that childhood cancers may be more common among those who received injected Vitamin K at the time of birth. The advice now given is for paediatricians and midwives and other health care professionals to establish locally agreed policies regarding administration of Vitamin K. Oral Vitamin K is often the preferred method of administration now; however, there is no licensed preparation of Vitamin K for oral use available in the UK, so individual doctors have to take responsibility for its use.

(b) Studies have shown that the consumption of water containing 1ppm fluoride reduces the incidence of dental caries by up to 70 per cent. Therefore in areas where the fluoride content of tap water is less than 0.3ppm daily supplements of fluoride are recommended during the period of tooth development. Fluoride drops and tablets should be stored out of reach of children and over-dosage should be avoided as this can cause mottling of the teeth.

(c) The DOH recommends that vitamin supplements are given to infants and young children from the age of six months until at least two years and preferably five years. Earlier introduction is justified only if the breastfeeding mother has a poor vitamin status or if the baby was premature.

Possible contaminants of breast milk

Your baby will be taking in small amounts of whatever you are consuming. Care needs to be taken by you in relation to the following substances.

CAFFEINE

Caffeine passes quickly into breast milk and will affect the baby in the same way it affects you. More than six to eight cups a day of caffeine-containing drinks, such as coffee, tea, cocoa and cola, can cause accumulation of caffeine in a breastfed baby and this in turn may cause abnormal activity and sleeplessness. This will disappear after a few days if the mother eliminates caffeine from her diet. Smoking increases the effects of caffeine.

ALCOHOL

Alcohol also passes quickly into your breast milk and the more you drink the more your baby will receive. Even the equivalent of one pint of beer can alter the smell of your breast milk and reduce the amount of milk that your baby receives during the following three hours. Some babies are also temporarily uncomfortable and irritable after their mother has had a drink. If you drink enough to make you feel 'tipsy', this may affect your hormone balance and cause the letdown reflex to be unreliable.

NICOTINE

Breastfeeding women who smoke are more likely to have babies who cry a lot and develop 'colic'. Heavy smoking (more than twenty cigarettes a day) may not only decrease the milk supply and interfere with the letdown reflex but may also cause nausea and vomiting in the baby. Inhaling cigarette smoke increases a baby's risk of getting lung disorders such as bronchiolitis and pneumonia and puts him or her at greater risk of dying from sudden infant death syndrome.

ILLEGAL DRUGS

Smoking marijuana also interferes with the letdown reflex and the compound 9-tetrahydrocannabinol from marijuana smoke has also been found in samples of breast milk. Heroin, cocaine and other such 'hard drugs' would be very unsafe for breastfed babies to come into contact with via their breast milk.

MEDICATIONS

As a general rule, if you don't have to take the drug or medication, don't. A certain amount of any drug that you swallow, sniff, inhale, insert (in your anus or vagina) or inject will get into your breast milk, though on average no more than 1 or 2 per cent of the maternal dose. Many will be harmless to the baby but there are some which, even in minute amounts, can be damaging. So if you have to take a medication always check with your doctor or pharmacist that it is safe to take it while you are breastfeeding.

ORAL CONTRACEPTIVES

There is no evidence that the progesterone-only pill (the 'mini' pill) affects the baby in any way. The ordinary pill (containing oestrogen and progesterone) can, however, reduce the milk supply.

PESTICIDES AND OTHER ENVIRONMENTAL CONTAMINANTS

The current concerns about pesticide residues, industrial wastes and other environmental contaminants are not without cause. Long-term low-level exposure results in gradual accumulation of residues in animal and human fat; breast milk therefore gets contaminated by the fat we eat and the fat in our bodies which is being mobilized to make it. However, at the present concentrations reported in breast milk the possible risks are outweighed by the advantages of breastfeeding and there is no justification for either limiting breastfeeding or eliminating specific food items from the diet. Other sources of contamination, such as occupational exposure and using pesticides in gardens and homes, should be kept to a minimum.

Expressing, storing and reheating breast milk

You may find that you need to express your milk, for example if your baby has to be treated in the hospital special care unit and is not able to breastfeed initially, or because you have to return to work. Also one of the disadvantages of breastfeeding often quoted is that no one else, in particular the father, can share in the pleasure of feeding the baby and in turn this also means that you cannot leave your baby for longer than an hour or two. By learning to express your breast milk, however, this possible disadvantage can easily be overcome.

You can express milk by hand or by pump; the midwife or health visitor will give you instruction and advice. Hand expression can be done anywhere, any time and at no cost, and it requires only basic bodily cleanliness and thorough cleaning of milk containers. Using a pump, either hand or electric, is usually faster than hand expression but the pump must be carefully cleaned after every use. Electric pumps are fairly expensive but can be hired through the National Childbirth Trust or some hospitals.

Expressed breast milk can be stored for twenty-four hours in a refrigerator in a sterile bottle. It can also be frozen for future use in a sterile bottle or plastic bag; in a separate freezer it can keep for three months, but if kept in the small freezing space within the refrigerator it should be used within two weeks. Do not store breast milk in the rack in the refrigerator or freezer door; keep it at the back where it is coldest.

Never refreeze milk after it has thawed, and do not use a microwave oven to thaw or warm frozen milk. It does not heat evenly and can overheat milk in the centre of the bottle. It also destroys Vitamin C. Just leave frozen milk to thaw naturally or overnight in the refrigerator and take the chill off the milk by standing it in a saucepan of hot water.

BOTTLE FEEDING

Hygiene considerations of bottle feeding

If you are bottle feeding your baby, either with breast milk or formula milk, it is very important that all equipment is washed and sterilized before use to protect your baby against the possibility of infection.

As soon as possible after use, empty the bottle and rinse with cold water. Bottles, teats and other equipment should then be washed thoroughly in hot soapy water. A bottle brush should be used, and there are now teat brushes available, or you can turn the teat inside out to make sure the hole is not clogged. Everything should then be rinsed in clean running water before sterilization. There are three methods of sterilization:

1 *Cold water sterilization*
Fill a sterilizing tank (or other large plastic container with lid, such as an ice-cream container) with cold water. Add the recommended amount of sterilizing tablets or solution, ensuring that the tablet is completely dissolved. Put bottles, teats and other equipment (but nothing metal) into the water. Use the floating lid of the sterilizing unit or a large plate to keep everything under the water. Make sure there are no air bubbles trapped in the bottles. Leave for the time given in the instructions. If sterilizing daily, a fresh solution should be made up every twenty-four hours.

2 *Boiling water sterilization*
Place bottles and caps in a large saucepan (it is best to keep one specifically for this purpose). Fill the pan with water, completely immersing everything and making sure there are no air bubbles. Boil for five minutes with the lid on. Add teats and continue boiling for a further five minutes. Allow to cool and leave covered with the saucepan lid until you are ready to use the equipment. (This method tends to wear out the teats, so check them regularly and replace them when they become swollen and spongy.)

3   *Steam sterilization*

Place all the items into an electrical sterilizer. Add the required water. Close the lid and switch on. The cycle usually lasts about twelve minutes. You do not need to rinse the bottles afterwards.

Other hygiene and safety considerations involved in bottle feeding concern the making up of formula feeds. These include:

i)   Use cooled (about 50°C), recently boiled water for making up feeds. Do not use repeatedly boiled water, filtered water or artificially softened water. If using bottled mineral water get advice from your health visitor or pharmacist first to ensure that the brand you use is suitable for babies. (Bottled mineral water is not sterilized so it needs to be boiled first.)

ii)   Wash, rinse and dry hands thoroughly before making up a feed.

iii) Use measuring marks on the side of the bottle to fill the bottle with the correct amount of water. Always put the water in first.

iv)   Measure exact amount of powder using the scoop provided with each container of milk. Do not press the powder down. Too much powder will over-concentrate the feed and will be harmful for your baby.

v)   Do not add anything else to the feed, for example sugar, honey, rusk, or cereal.

vi)   Put cap on and shake thoroughly until all the powder has dissolved.

vii) Test the temperature of the feed by dripping a little on to the inside of your wrist. It should feel slightly warm. If the bottle has just come out of the fridge, take the chill off it by standing it in a saucepan of hot water. Do not use a microwave oven, it can overheat the milk in the centre of the bottle and scald the baby.

Brands and types of baby milks

There are a number of different brands of baby milks on sale in the shops. You can also buy milk at your child health clinic, usually more cheaply. Use one of the recognized formulas which comply with Department of Health guidelines. Those available at present in the UK are listed below.

Infant Formulas

Manufacturer	Whey-based brand	Curd-based brand
Wyeth	SMA	Gold SMA
Cow and Gate	Premium	Premium Plus
Farley	Oster Milk	Oster Milk II
Milupa	Aptamil	Milumil

The whey-based milks are more suitable for the younger bottle-fed baby as their composition more closely resembles that of breast milk. The curd- or casein-based milks have higher levels of protein and minerals then the whey-based milks, and they contain a much higher proportion of the curd protein which takes longer for the baby to digest.

Approved soya formulas are also available for babies who cannot tolerate formulas based on cow's milk (due to cow's milk protein allergy or lactose intolerance), e.g. Wysoy, Formula S, Oster Soy, Isomil and Pro-Sobee, but consult your doctor first if you suspect this. These are available on prescription for established forms of cows' milk intolerance.

Infant formulas contain vitamins so you will probably not be advised to give your baby vitamin drops as well.

If you are on Income Support, you can claim tokens for free milk and vitamins for your baby. Take your certificate of pregnancy (form FW8) to your local Social Security office.

INFANT COLIC AND INFANT ALLERGIES

Colic

Infant colic occurs fairly commonly in the first three months after birth, the symptoms being that a baby draws up its legs, screams and cries, indicative of acute abdominal pain. The causes of colic can sometimes be attributed to hunger, the swallowing of air, or food allergy, but in many cases the problem goes away without a reason being found for it.

There is no scientific evidence to support the idea that lactating mothers in general should avoid certain fruits or vegetables or gas-forming foods. However, caffeine, cocoa and cows' milk have been reported to produce colicky behaviour in some infants, and if you suspect that your baby is reacting to a certain food that you are eating, try omitting it from your diet for a couple of days. If symptoms improve, either continue to omit it, if it's a non-essential like chocolate, or try it out again to see if the colic recurs. If you find that it's a food that forms an important part of your diet, you should seek advice. In many cultures highly spiced food is avoided during lactation because it is thought that it would upset the baby. There have been no studies to look into this.

Cow's milk intolerance

It is estimated that 3 per cent of infants are allergic to cow's milk. Reactions include symptoms such as diarrhoea, vomiting or colic, skin rashes such as eczema and breathing problems such as asthma. If you suspect that your baby is allergic, you should seek medical advice. Management would involve the substitution of cow's milk or cow's milk infant formula with one of the soya-based infant formulas such as Cow and Gate Formula S, Pro-Sobee, Isomil, Oster Soy, or Wysoy. These can be obtained on prescription in the UK if a diagnosis of cow's milk allergy has been established. In very severe cases of cow's milk allergy where damage to the absorptive surface of the intestine has occurred or in cases where there is also a soya allergy, formulas in which the protein has been pre-digested (hydrolysed) can be prescribed. Pregestimil (Mead Johnson) is suitable for infants under six months and Nutramigen (Mead Johnson) for older babies and children. These should be used only on medical advice.

Eczema and asthma

Eczema and asthma (recurrent wheezing or coughing) are the most common allergic disorders seen in infancy. Both food allergens (for example, cow's milk and other dairy products, eggs, fish, nuts, soya beans) and environmental allergens (for example, tree and grass pollen, house-dust mites and animal danders) may sensitize a vulnerable infant and initiate the development of allergic reactions.

At present prevention measures are advocated only for high-risk infants, i.e. those born into families with a strong history of allergy. Mothers are advised to:

(a) breastfeed (exclusively, if possible) or, if unable to, to substitute with a hypoallergenic formula, for example Aptamil H A

(b) avoid dairy products, eggs, fish, nuts and possibly other common food allergens whilst lactating (and obtain dietary advice to ensure adequate intakes of protein, minerals and vitamins)

(c) delay the introduction of solid foods until their baby is 5–6 months old

(d) avoid introducing strong antigenic foods during the first year.

Maternal avoidance of foods during pregnancy has not been shown to have any benefits.

There is some debate as to whether these measures prevent, reduce or simply delay the development of allergic disorders. However, it is felt they are justified even if the outcome is only a delay.

There are, in addition, at least 35 per cent of children with obvious allergic diseases who do not have a positive family history of allergy and this perhaps adds weight to the general advice for all mothers to breastfeed if possible, to delay introducing solid foods until 5–6 months and to avoid introducing highly allergenic foods until the latter part of the first year.

MATERNAL WEIGHT LOSS AFTER THE BIRTH

Many women hope for a rapid return to their pre-pregnancy body weight. However, this is rare and efforts to achieve it by dieting are likely both to be incompatible with the successful initiation of breastfeeding and to increase the tiredness commonly felt when you are caring for a new baby. It may be helpful to remember that it took nine months for your body to lay down the extra fat and tissue during pregnancy and you should therefore expect it to take a similar length of time to mobilize and expend it. It may take even longer than this as recent studies suggest that during the first two months after delivery the body is still in its 'energy-efficient' mode and is not utilizing its pregnancy fat stores.

Having said this, you will probably find that the most rapid weight loss occurs during the first three months after the birth, due mainly to tissue and water losses. A recent study on Swedish women found them to have lost on average 11 kg three months after delivery and to be about 3 kg (7 lb) heavier than their (self-reported) pre-pregnancy weight. Weight loss thereafter was much slower and at one year after delivery they were on average 1.5 kg (3 lb) heavier than their pre-pregnancy weight. The researchers concluded that the true average weight gain was in fact likely to be less than this as the self-reported pre-pregnancy weights were probably under-estimated. However, what this study also showed was the wide variation in weight change – 20 per cent of women had actually decreased their weight one year after the birth, compared to pre-pregnancy, and 29 per cent had gained 3 kg (7 lb) or more. A small proportion of the women (2.3 per cent) had increased their weight by 9 kg (20 lb) or more.

The factor which was found to be most strongly associated with weight retention was high weight gain during pregnancy, which is why it is important to try not to exceed the recommended pregnancy weight gain for your particular weight and height proportions (see page 49). Women who stopped smoking during pregnancy were more likely to be amongst the group of women who gained excessive weight during pregnancy and had increased weight retention after delivery, which is why it is important to try to stop smoking before pregnancy. Other lifestyle changes may also influence weight retention in the period after delivery, for example, whether and when you choose to return to work outside the home. One study has found that women who return to work outside the home sooner have a lower weight retention; this is perhaps because women who are not in paid work have access to food throughout the day and spend more time cooking and feeding others. Also the degree of exercise and general activity may not return to the level you were accustomed to pre-pregnancy. Whether or not you breastfeed and for how long may also affect weight retention but opinions on this are divided. Some studies have found no difference with method of feeding; the Swedish study found that breastfeeding had the largest effect on weight loss between ten weeks and six months after the birth, but that a long-term effect of lactation on weight loss (one year after the birth) was observed only in a small group who practised very intensive and lengthy lactation.

Our advice on trying to ensure a return to your pre-pregnancy weight, or near to it, is to carry on or begin following healthy living patterns, including eating healthily (see Chapter 4) and exercising regularly, taking particular care if you find you are either putting on weight or you are getting stuck at a weight that is above the range for your height (see tables on pages 10 and 11).

EXERCISE AFTER THE BIRTH

Many women will be familiar with recommended exercise programmes for the first few days after delivery which are designed to strengthen the back and the abdominal muscles as well as helping with the muscles of the pelvis which are naturally stretched during the birth process.

As for returning to a pre-pregnancy exercise programme, this should probably be deferred for about six weeks to allow the joints and ligaments to tighten up and get back to their previous strength and positions. Thereafter exercise programmes can be reintroduced and built up slowly. It is particularly important not to overdo things whilst breastfeeding because, as with drastic dieting, your milk supply will be affected. Whilst breastfeeding the breasts may be rather uncomfortable during exercise and you will need a well-designed and supportive bra.

Meal Plans and Recipes

IDEAS FOR MEALS RICH IN IRON AND VITAMIN C

It is always worth remembering that taking Vitamin C in combination with iron will increase the amount of iron you absorb from your food. Also that the tannin in tea decreases iron absorption, so try to drink it in between meals rather than during them.

BREAKFASTS

An easy way of increasing your iron absorption from your breakfast is to include a glass of fruit juice – orange or grapefruit in particular are very rich in Vitamin C. You could also try fruit juice on cereal instead of milk. Here are some examples of breakfasts which include good sources of iron and Vitamin C.

1   Glass of fruit juice
Breakfast cereal with milk
High-fibre white toast with butter or margarine

2   Porridge with milk
Grilled bacon and tomato
Wholemeal toast with butter or margarine

3   Weetabix with fresh orange juice and sliced banana
Boiled egg
Toast with butter or margarine

LUNCHES

Salads containing Vitamin C-rich vegetables taken with meat, egg or pulses will increase the iron absorbed from these foods. Jacket potatoes contain both iron and Vitamin C. Dried fruits also contain iron. Some examples follow. Recipes for those marked with an asterisk appear on pages 161 to 163.

1   Mixed bean salad*
    Tomato and cucumber salad
    Wholemeal bread
    1 apple

2   Ham/salami and green pepper pizza*
    Lettuce and avocado salad
    1 orange

3   Jacket potato
    Baked beans
    Tinned guavas

4   Pilchards in tomato sauce
    Wholemeal toast
    Melon

DINNERS

As with lunches, Vitamin C-rich vegetables will increase the iron absorbed from your meal.

1   Spinach and cauliflower bhaji*
    Brown rice

2   Steak and vegetable stir-fry*
    Noodles

3   Kidney, bacon and green pepper kebabs*
    Jacket potato and salad

4   Lentil and red pepper sauce*
    Pasta and watercress salad

Recipes for meals rich in iron and Vitamin C

MIXED BEAN SALAD
serves 6–8

110 g (4 oz) butter beans
110 g (4 oz) red kidney beans
pinch of salt
110 g (4 oz) French beans, cut into 2.5 cm (1 in) lengths
6 spring onions, chopped
4 tbsp French dressing
2 tbsp parsley, chopped

Soak the beans separately overnight. Drain, place in separate pans, cover with cold water, bring to the boil and boil steadily for 15 minutes. Lower the heat, cover and simmer for 1–1½ hours, adding a little salt towards the end of the cooking time. (Alternatively, use canned beans).

Cook the French beans in boiling water for 7–8 minutes, then drain.

Place all the beans in a bowl, and mix in the onions and dressing while warm. Leave to cool.

Stir in the parsley and transfer to a salad bowl to serve.

SPINACH AND CAULIFLOWER BHAJI
[quick method using frozen vegetables]
serves 4

225 g (8 oz) frozen leaf spinach
225 g (8 oz) frozen cauliflower florets
225 g (8 oz) frozen sliced courgettes
1 medium onion, peeled and sliced
2 cloves of garlic, crushed
1–2 tbsp sunflower oil or olive oil
1 tsp garam masala

1 tsp mustard seeds
1–2 tbsp thick set natural yoghurt

Place the frozen spinach in a bowl, cover with boiling water and leave to thaw for 2–3 minutes. Squeeze dry through a sieve, pressing with large spoon. Set aside. Place the cauliflower and courgettes in a large saucepan, cover with boiling water and simmer for 6 minutes. Strain.

Fry the garlic, onion, mustard seeds and garam masala in the oil over a low heat for 3–4 minutes. Add the spinach, cauliflower and courgettes, toss evenly, cover and continue to cook for a further 15 minutes. Just before serving stir in the yoghurt.

STEAK AND VEGETABLE STIR FRY
serves 4

2 tbsp sunflower or olive oil
1–2 cloves garlic, crushed
$\frac{1}{2}$ tsp ground ginger
1 medium onion, peeled and sliced
350 g (12 $\frac{1}{4}$ oz) rump steak, cut in strips
3 sticks of celery, chopped
170 g (6 oz) carrots, cut in strips
170 g (6 oz) cabbage, sliced
110 g (4 oz) mushrooms, sliced
1 small red pepper, cut into strips
1 orange
black pepper

Heat the oil in a wok or deep frying pan. Add the garlic, ginger and onion and stir fry until the onion is golden. Add the beef and other vegetables and stir fry until the meat is evenly browned.

Segment the orange over a bowl to catch the juice. Add both to the pan, cover and simmer for 3 minutes, stirring from time to time. Season with black pepper to taste.

KIDNEY, BACON AND GREEN PEPPER KEBABS
serves 4

12 rashers streaky bacon, derinded
2 green peppers, chopped
12 lambs' kidneys
6 small onions
2 tbsp olive oil
1 tbsp thyme leaves
$\frac{1}{4}$ tsp black pepper

Cut the bacon rashers in half and roll up. Cut the peppers into 24 pieces. Skin, core and halve the kidneys. Cut the onions into quarters. Thread the kidney, bacon, onion and pepper alternately on to 8 skewers. Mix the oil and thyme with the pepper; brush over the kebabs. Cook under a preheated hot grill for 8–10 minutes, turning and basting with the oil mixture frequently.

LENTIL AND RED PEPPER SAUCE
serves 4

1 onion, peeled and chopped
1 small red pepper, chopped
2 tbsp olive oil
1 garlic clove, crushed
1 tsp dried basil
225 g (8 oz) can tomatoes
124 g (4$\frac{1}{4}$ oz) split red lentils
1 tsp tomato purée
400 ml ($\frac{3}{4}$ pt) water, salted
black pepper
sugar
grated cheese (optional)

Fry the onion and pepper in the oil in a large saucepan for 10 minutes, then put in the garlic, basil, tomatoes, lentils, tomato purée and salted water. Bring to the boil, then lower the heat and leave to simmer gently, uncovered, for 15–20 minutes, until the lentils are cooked. Season with pepper and a dash of sugar. Top with grated cheese.

IDEAS FOR MEALS RICH IN CALCIUM

Calcium-rich meals obviously include those in which there is a plentiful supply of milk or cheese. For those who do not eat dairy products, soya milk (enriched with calcium) and non-dairy cheese are now available and can be used in place of dairy products in most recipes.

Seeds (especially sesame), nuts, whole cereals, beans, peas, dried fruit (especially figs) and molasses and dark treacle are also good sources of calcium. Sardines and pilchards are useful sources for non-vegetarians (check Table 14 in Appendix 2 for the best sources).

Recipes for meals marked with an asterisk appear on pages 165 to 168.

BREAKFASTS

1　Cereals/porridge with milk/soya milk/sesame seed milk (made from ground and blended sesame seeds)

2　Toast spread with mixture of tahini and dark treacle

LUNCHES

1　Cheese sandwich

2　Jacket potato with cheese topping

3　Tahini dip* with toast, celery and cucumber slices

4　Sardines on toast

5　Hazelnut spread* sandwich

DINNERS

1   Quiche/pizza

2   Nut roast*

3   Tofu and mushroom flan*

4   Vegetables with cheese sauce*

5   Tofu fritters*

Serve with pasta, rice, a jacket potato, or bread, and a selection of vegetables. Broccoli, watercress and spinach are the vegetables most rich in calcium. Dishes 1–3 can also be served cold with a salad.

Recipes for meals rich in calcium

TAHINI DIP
serves 4

2 heaped tbsp tahini (sesame paste)
1 clove garlic, crushed
$\frac{1}{2}$ tsp salt
1–2 tbsp parsley, finely chopped
2–3 tbsp lemon juice
a little water, if necessary

Mix all the ingredients together, adding a little water if needed, to make a smooth cream. Serve with toast, celery and cucumber pieces.

HAZELNUT SPREAD
Makes about 225 g (8 oz)

110 g (4 oz) hazelnuts
110 g (4 oz) sunflower seeds

15 g (½ oz) polyunsaturated margarine
4 tbsp hot water
1 garlic clove, crushed
1 tbsp soy sauce
salt and black pepper

Toast the nuts and sunflower seeds under a hot grill or in a moderate oven. If the nuts still have brown skins on, remove these after toasting by rubbing the nuts gently in a soft, clean cloth. Grind the nuts and sunflower seeds finely in a coffee grinder or blender, then mix with the margarine, water, garlic and soy sauce. Beat until smooth and creamy. Season with salt and pepper.

Nut Roast
serves 4

55 g (2 oz) crushed almonds
55 g (2 oz) crushed cashew nuts
110 g (4 oz) crushed Brazil nuts
1 small onion fried in 25 g (1 oz) butter or oil
2 tbsp wheatgerm
110 g (4 oz) tomatoes, skinned and sliced or small tin of
tomatoes, drained and chopped
2 eggs
1 level tsp mixed herbs or thyme
salt and black pepper to taste

Mix all the ingredients together well. Pack into a greased ovenproof dish or tin. Brush the top with melted butter or oil. Bake on the top shelf of the oven preheated to 180°C/350°F/Gas Mark 4 for 40 minutes until brown. Serve hot with gravy or onion sauce, greens and potatoes, or cold, sliced with salad, chips or rolls and butter.

TOFU AND MUSHROOM FLAN
serves 4

110 g (4 oz) self-raising flour
pinch of salt
65 g (2¼ oz) polyunsaturated margarine
1 onion, peeled and finely chopped
25 g (1 oz) vegetable margarine
1 garlic clove, crushed
110 g (4 oz) white button mushrooms, washed and thinly sliced
300 g (10½ oz) packet tofu
salt and black pepper
25 g (1 oz) ground almonds

Preheat oven to 190°C/375°F/Gas Mark 5. Grease a 20-cm (8-in) round flan tin or dish. Sift the flour and salt into a bowl. Rub in the margarine until the mixture looks like fine breadcrumbs. Gently press together to make a dough (no water is needed). Place the dough on a lightly floured board and knead into a circle. Roll out thinly and lift into a flan dish. Trim the edges. Fry the onion gently in the margarine until soft, then put in the garlic and mushrooms and cook for a further 3 minutes. Remove from the heat and stir in the tofu. Season with salt and pepper. Spoon into a flan case, level the top, and sprinkle with ground almonds. Bake for 40 minutes until the pastry is crisp and golden brown and puffed up.

CHEESE SAUCE
serves 4

80 g (2¾ oz) butter or polyunsaturated margarine
80 g (2¾ oz) unbleached white flour
900 ml (1½ pt) milk or soya milk
1 bay leaf
salt and black pepper
55–110 g (2–4 oz) grated cheese/tofu cheese
pinch of dry mustard powder or cayenne pepper

Melt the butter or margarine, then stir in the flour. Cool for 1 minute, then add a third of the milk and stir until thickened; repeat with another third, then finally add the rest, together with the bay leaf and seasoning. Stir over a moderate heat until thickened. Simmer gently for 10 minutes to cook the flour. Stir the cheese and mustard powder or cayenne pepper into the cooked sauce. Pour over cooked pasta and boiled vegetables of your choice.

TOFU FRITTERS
serves 4

2 × 300 g (10½ oz) packets tofu
salt and black pepper
lemon juice
wholewheat flour
sunflower oil for frying
1 lemon cut into wedges

Carefully drain the tofu so as not to break it up. Wrap each block in a clean absorbent cloth. Place in a colander and weight it down. Leave for several hours or overnight to drain and firm up, then cut into slices, sprinkle each with salt, pepper and a few drops of lemon juice and coat in flour. Shallow fry until crisp and golden brown on both sides. Drain on kitchen paper. Serve at once, with the lemon wedges, a yoghurt dressing and a salad or cooked vegetables.

IDEAS FOR PROTEIN COMPLEMENTATION MEALS

For vegans or vegetarians or those who do not eat animal protein foods often it is important to ensure that the mixture of protein foods they eat are complementary, so that they obtain adequate amounts of the essential amino acids. This basically means that pulses should be combined with cereals, nuts or oil seeds, although it is not essential that this is done at every meal.

Recipes for meals marked with an asterisk appear on the following few pages, with the exception of 'mixed bean salad', the recipe for which is on page 161.

BREAKFASTS

1   Breakfast cereals with soya or sesame seed milk
2   Wholemeal toast with peanut butter

LUNCHES

1   Baked beans on toast
2   Hummous* with bread
3   Bean/lentil soup* with bread
4   Bean and pasta salad (mix cooked pasta with mixed bean salad*)

DINNERS

1   Rice with lentil dahl* (plus vegetables)
2   Vegetarian lasagne* (beans instead of mince)
3   Butter bean and vegetable casserole* with rice or buckwheat
4   Lentil and onion cutlets* with new potatoes and salad
5   Chilli red kidney beans* with rice

Recipes for protein complementation meals

HUMMOUS
serves 4–6

110 g (4 oz) chick peas, soaked overnight
salt and black pepper

2 tbsp tahini (sesame paste)
1–2 cloves garlic, crushed
juice of ½ lemon
2 tbsp olive oil

Drain the chick peas, place in a pan and cover with cold water. Bring to the boil and simmer gently for 2–2½ hours until soft, adding a little salt towards the end of cooking.

Drain, reserving 120 ml (4 fl oz) of the liquid. Place the chick peas in an electric blender with the tahini, garlic, lemon juice, oil, reserved liquid, ½ teaspoon salt and ¼ teaspoon pepper. Blend to a soft creamy purée. Serve with wholemeal bread.

Lentil Soup
serves 4

1 onion, peeled and chopped
15 g (½ oz) butter or margarine
1 garlic clove, crushed
225 g (8 oz) split red lentils
1.2 litres (2 pt) water
1–2 tbsp lemon juice
salt and black pepper

Fry the onion gently in the butter or margarine for 10 minutes, until softened. Add the garlic, lentils and water. Bring to the boil, then simmer for 15–20 minutes, until the lentils are soft. Add lemon juice and seasoning to taste.

Bean Soup
serves 4

2 large onions, chopped
2 tbsp olive oil
350 g (12¼ oz) home-cooked beans of your choice, e.g. butter beans, cannellini beans, black-eyed beans or haricot beans.
(Alternatively, use canned beans)

425 g (15 oz) can tomatoes
1 tbsp tomato purée
salt and black pepper
sugar

Fry the onions gently in the oil for 10 minutes until soft. Drain the beans, reserving the liquid, and return to the pan. Add the beans and tomatoes to the onion. Make the reserved liquid up to 300 ml (10 fl oz) with water and add to the pan, together with the tomato purée. Cook gently for about 5 minutes, until everything is heated through. Season with salt, pepper and a little sugar.

Lentil Dahl
serves 4

1 medium onion, chopped
225 g (8 oz) lentils
3–4 tbsp sunflower oil
1–2 tbsp curry powder
600 ml (1 pt) water
1 tsp yeast extract
25 g (1 oz) coconut cream
1 tbsp tomato purée
salt
few chopped chives

Fry the onion with the lentils in the oil over a low heat for 5 minutes. Stir in the curry powder, water, yeast extract, coconut cream and tomato purée. Bring to the boil and simmer over a low heat until the lentils are tender and liquid is absorbed. Stir occasionally with a spoon handle or fork so the lentils are not mashed. Add more water if needed, and salt to taste. Turn into a hot serving dish and garnish with chives. Serve with rice.

VEGETARIAN LASAGNE
serves 4

1 tbsp sunflower oil
225 g (8 oz) onion, chopped
110 g (4 oz) mushroom, sliced
425 g (15 oz) can baked beans *or* other beans of choice
2 tbsp tomato purée
150 ml (¼ pt) vegetable stock
850 ml (1½ pt) milk
55 g (2 oz) margarine
55 g (2 oz) flour
salt and black pepper
110 g (4 oz) grated cheese
12 sheets wholewheat lasagne

Gently fry the onions in the oil until softened. Add the mushrooms and cook for a further minute. Add the beans, tomato purée and stock and mix well together. Put to one side.

Melt the margarine in a saucepan and mix in the flour. Cook gently for 1 minute. Gradually add the milk, stirring continuously until the mixture thickens. Season to taste and add 75 g (3 oz) cheese. Mix well.

Spoon a thin layer of bean mixture and a little cheese sauce over the base of a 23-cm (9-in) square ovenproof dish. Cover with four slices of lasagne. Repeat twice more. Cover with the remaining cheese sauce and sprinkle with grated cheese. Cook in an oven preheated to 190°C/375°F/Gas Mark 5 for approximately 35 minutes, until the top is browned.

BUTTER BEAN AND VEGETABLE CASSEROLE
serves 4

2 large onions
2 tbsp oil
900 g (2 lb) mixed root vegetables (carrot, swede, turnip, celery),
cut into even-sized pieces

2 tbsp plain flour
175 g (6 ¼oz) butter beans, soaked for 6–8 hrs, drained and
rinsed. (Alternatively, use canned beans)
900 ml (1½ pt) water
2 vegetable stock cubes
1–2 tbsp soy sauce
salt and black pepper
chopped parsley

Fry the onion in the oil for 5 minutes, then add the vegetables
and stir for a minute or two. Sprinkle in the flour and mix with
the vegetables, then add the butter beans, water and stock cubes.
Simmer gently for 1–1½ hours, stirring occasionally, until the
vegetables and beans are tender, or bake in an oven preheated to
160°C/325°F/Gas Mark 3 for 1½ hours. Add the soy sauce and
season to taste. Sprinkle with chopped parsley.

LENTIL AND ONION CUTLETS
makes 20

500 g (1 lb) split red lentils
850 ml (1½ pt) water
4 bay leaves
3 large onions, peeled and finely chopped
4 tbsp sunflower oil
3–4 tbsp lemon juice
salt and black pepper
wholewheat flour for coating
oil for shallow frying

Put the lentils into a pan with the water and bay leaves. Bring to
the boil, then cover and turn the heat down. Cook gently for
15–20 minutes until soft. Meanwhile, fry the onions in the oil for
10 minutes, until softened. Add the onions to the lentils and mix
well, mashing the lentils. Add the lemon juice and salt and
pepper to taste. Form into cutlet shapes and coat with wholewheat flour. Shallow fry in a little oil, treating them gently.

Serve with a yoghurt dressing and a salad, or gravy and mixed vegetables.

Chilli Red Kidney Beans
serves 4

1 onion, peeled and chopped
1 red pepper, chopped
2 tbsp sunflower oil
425 g (15 oz) canned tomatoes
425 g (15 oz) canned red kidney beans *or* home-cooked beans
1 tsp chilli powder
salt and black pepper

Fry the onion and red pepper gently in the oil for 10 minutes, then add the tomatoes, red kidney beans, chilli powder and salt and pepper to taste. Stir over a gentle heat for 5–10 minutes, until the beans are heated through. Serve with brown rice.

IDEAS FOR NUTRIENT-RICH LOW-COST MEALS

If money is tight, try not to skimp on meals. It is really important to eat properly and although using mostly fresh foods involves a bit more effort and time spent cooking, it is usually cheaper and more nutritious.

Recipes for meals marked with an asterisk appear on pages 176 to 178, with the exception of 'cheese sauce', the recipe for which is on page 167.

BREAKFASTS

Fortified breakfast cereals with milk can provide significant amounts of many important nutrients such as iron, calcium, zinc and some of the B vitamins. Wholemeal toast and high-fibre enriched white bread are more nutrient-dense than ordinary white bread. Eggs once or twice a week can provide extra protein, iron, zinc, Vitamin A and some of the B vitamins.

LUNCHES

1   Jacket potato with baked beans, grated cheese, cottage cheese, tuna and mayonnaise or other favourite topping

2   Sardines on toast

3   Celery and potato soup* (use other vegetables as replacement for celery if you prefer) with bread

4   Ham/cheese/tuna fish/peanut butter sandwiches using wholewheat or high fibre white bread

Try to have some fresh salad vegetables and a piece of fruit or a yoghurt with your lunch.

DINNERS

1   Macaroni and boiled vegetables covered with cheese sauce*

2   Minced lamb and vegetables in tomato sauce* with spaghetti

3   Lancashire hotpot* with boiled potatoes and carrots

4   Kidney stir fry* with brown rice or noodles

5   Bean and pork hotpot* with brown rice and broccoli

Many of the vegetarian recipes mentioned in previous sections will also be very economical dishes.

DESSERTS AND CAKES

Stewed fruit with custard, semolina or natural yoghurt can provide a simple nutritious dessert. Homemade fruit cake or gingerbread are cheaper and more healthy choices of cake than cream cake or pastries.

Recipes for low-cost meals

CELERY AND POTATO SOUP
serves 4

2 tbsp sunflower oil
2 medium onions, chopped
4 sticks celery, sliced
4 medium potatoes, peeled and cut into small cubes
2 medium carrots, peeled and sliced
1200 ml (2 pt) vegetable or chicken stock
black pepper to taste

Place the oil in a large saucepan. Fry the onion, celery and carrot for about 5 minutes. Add the potato, stock and pepper and bring to the boil. Reduce the heat, cover and simmer for 20 minutes until the vegetables are tender. If you want a creamy soup, sieve it or use a blender.

MINCED LAMB AND VEGETABLES IN TOMATO SAUCE
serves 4

335 g (¾ lb) minced lamb
1 medium onion, chopped
1 clove garlic, crushed
1 medium carrot, chopped
1 green pepper, chopped
50 g (1¾ oz) mushrooms, sliced
200 g (7 oz) can tomatoes
2 tbsp tomato purée
½ tsp dried oregano
salt and black pepper

Put the minced lamb into a cold saucepan and heat gently until some fat runs out. Increase the heat and fry until brown. Drain off any excess fat and add the onion, garlic, carrots and pepper and fry until the vegetables are soft. Add the mushrooms and fry for a further 2 minutes. Stir in the tomatoes with the juice, tomato purée, oregano and seasoning, adding additional water to cover if necessary. Bring to the boil, cover and simmer for 30 minutes. Serve on top of spaghetti.

LANCASHIRE HOTPOT
serves 4

550 g (1 ¼ lb) trimmed middle neck lamb chops
seasoned flour
4 tbsp sunflower oil
2 onions, sliced
4 small carrots, sliced
2 large potatoes, sliced
250 ml (½ pt) stock
salt and black pepper

Coat the lamb in seasoned flour and brown in the oil. Place the lamb, onions, carrots and potatoes in a large casserole dish in alternate layers, finishing with an overlapping layer of potatoes. Pour in enough stock to come just below the top layer of potatoes. Cook in an oven preheated to 180°C/350°F/Gas Mark 4 for 2 hours. Remove the lid 40 minutes before the end of cooking time, to brown the potatoes.

KIDNEY STIR FRY
serves 4

335 g (¾ lb) lambs' kidneys, skinned, cored and cut into quarters
2 cloves garlic, crushed
2 tbsp sunflower oil
1 medium onion, sliced
2 carrots, cut into thin strips
165 g (5¾ oz) frozen whole green beans, chopped
pinch cayenne pepper
salt and black pepper
1 tbsp soy sauce

Fry the kidneys and garlic in the oil in a wok or heavy-based frying pan for 5 minutes. Add the rest of the ingredients and fry for a further 10 minutes, stirring continuously. Serve with brown rice or noodles.

BEAN AND PORK HOTPOT
serves 4

110 g (4 oz) haricot beans, soaked overnight
110 g (4 oz) red kidney beans, soaked overnight
165 g (5¾ oz) lean pork steak, diced
2 medium onions, sliced
2 cloves garlic, crushed
200 g (7 oz) can tomatoes, roughly chopped
2 tbsp tomato purée
few drops chilli sauce
1 tsp dry mustard
600 ml (1 pt) stock
black pepper to taste

Boil the beans for 10 minutes, reduce the heat and simmer for 40 minutes. Drain. Preheat the oven to 160°C/325°F/Gas Mark 3. Place the onion, garlic and tomatoes in a large casserole. Add the pork, drained beans and all remaining ingredients. Stir well, cover and cook for 1½ hours until the beans and meat are tender.

APPENDIX TWO

Tables showing Nutrient Content and Serving Size of a Selection of Foods

SELECTION OF FOODS

These tables include most commonly eaten foods, but we have, in the main, limited the foods selected to individual items rather than dishes which use a combination of foods.

PORTION SIZES

Most of the weights of portion sizes and the descriptions of them have been taken from the Royal Society of Chemistry's book *Nutrient Content of Food Portions*. These weights were determined by averaging three 'medium-sized' portions. As a result, the portions may not be equivalent to those you usually consume, i.e. they may be larger or smaller. Vegetarians, in particular, may find that the portion sizes for pulses used are less than the amounts they typically eat.

TABLE I
CALORIE CONTENT OF A SELECTION OF FOODS

	Description of serving	Weight	Calorie Content per serving
———————— STARCHY FOODS ————————			
Bread, crackers etc.			
Bread, wholemeal	2 slices, large loaf	75g (2¾oz)	151
Bread, white – high fibre	2 slices, large loaf	75g (2¾oz)	160
Bread, white	2 slices, large loaf	75g (2¾oz)	176
Naan	1 naan	170g (6oz)	571
Chapati, non-fat	1 (made without fat)	70g (2½oz)	141
Chapati	1 (made with fat)	70g (2½oz)	230
Pitta bread, wholemeal	1 pitta bread	65g (2¼oz)	172
Pitta bread, white	1 pitta bread	65g (2¼oz)	159
Rye crispbread	3 crispbreads	24g (1oz)	77
Cream crackers	3 crackers	21g (¾oz)	92
Scone, plain	1 scone	50g (1¾oz)	181
Pasta, rice, potatoes			
Pasta, wholemeal	6 tablespoons, cooked	150g (5¼oz)	170
Pasta, white	6 tablespoons, cooked	150g (5¼oz)	156
Rice, brown	4 tablespoons, cooked	165g (5¾oz)	233
Rice, white	4 tablespoons, cooked	165g (5¾oz)	203
Potato (baked)	1 large potato (with skin)	140g (5oz)	147
Potatoes (boiled)	4 tablespoons	150g (5¼oz)	120
Potatoes (roast)	2 medium potatoes	130g (4½oz)	204
Potatoes (chips)	chip shop portion	265g (9¼oz)	670
Oven chips	4 tablespoons	120g (4¼oz)	194
Sweet potato	2 medium, boiled	150g (5¼oz)	128

	Description of serving	Weight	Calorie Content per serving
Yam	⅙ average yam, boiled	130g (4½oz)	155
Crisps	1 packet	30g (1oz)	160
Breakfast cereals			
All Bran	7 tablespoons	45g (1½oz)	113
Bran Flakes	7 tablespoons	45g (1½oz)	144
Muesli, no added sugar	6 tablespoons	95g (3¼oz)	348
Corn Flakes	6 tablespoons	35g (1¼oz)	89
Rice Krispies	9 tablespoons	35g (1¼oz)	129

VEGETABLES

Avocado pear	½ pear	130g (4½oz)	201
Beansprouts	1 cup	80g (2¾oz)	7
Broad beans	1 heaped tablespoon, boiled	75g (2¾oz)	36
Broccoli	2 spears, boiled	95g (3¼oz)	17
Brussels sprouts	11 sprouts, boiled	115g (4oz)	21
Cabbage	3 tablespoons, boiled	75g (2¾oz)	7
Carrots	2½ tablespoons, boiled	65g (2¼oz)	12
Cauliflower	10 florets, boiled	100g (3½oz)	9
Green beans	30 beans, boiled	105g (3¾oz)	20
Green pepper	¼ pepper (raw)	45g (1½oz)	7
Leeks	1 small leek, boiled	125g (4½oz)	30
Lettuce	2-4 leaves	30g (1oz)	4
Mushrooms, raw	10 button mushrooms	55g (2oz)	5
Mushrooms, fried	10 button mushrooms	55g (2oz)	116
Okra, fried	2½ tablespoons, stir-fried	50g (1¾oz)	170
Olives	9 black, weighed with stones	35g (1¼oz)	29
Onions, raw	1 tablespoon	30g (1oz)	7

	Description of serving	Weight	Calorie Content per serving
Onions, fried	1 tablespoon	40g (1½oz)	138
Parsnips	2½ tablespoons, boiled	110g (4oz)	62
Peas, frozen	2½ tablespoons, boiled	75g (2¾oz)	31
Red pepper	¼ pepper (raw)	45g (1½oz)	7
Spinach	2½ tablespoons, boiled	130g (4½oz)	39
Spring greens	3 tablespoons, boiled	75g (2¾oz)	8
Swede	3 tablespoons, boiled	120g (4¼oz)	22
Sweetcorn, tinned	2½ tablespoons	70g (2½oz)	53
Tomatoes	2 medium sized (raw)	150g (5¼oz)	21
Watercress	¼ bunch	15g (½oz)	2

FRUIT

	Description of serving	Weight	Calorie Content per serving
Apple	1 apple	120g (4¼oz)	42
Apricots, fresh	3 apricots	110g (4oz)	28
Apricots, dried	8 apricots	50g (1¾oz)	91
Banana	1 banana	135g (4¾oz)	63
Blackberries	15 blackberries	75g (2¾oz)	23
Figs, dried	4 figs	60g (2oz)	128
Gooseberries	11 gooseberries	70g (2½oz)	26
Grapefruit	½ grapefruit	140g (5oz)	15
Grapes (white/black)	small bunch	140g (5oz)	80
Guavas, tinned	6 halves	176g (6¼oz)	105
Lychees, tinned	10 lychees	150g (5¼oz)	102
Mango	1 mango	315g (11oz)	109
Melon, cantaloupe	¼ melon	180g (6¼oz)	54
Melon, honeydew	1 slice	190g (6¾oz)	25
Nectarine	1 nectarine	120g (4¼oz)	51
Orange	1 large orange	245g (8½oz)	64
Peach	1 peach	120g (4¼oz)	40
Pineapple, fresh	1 slice	126g (4½oz)	58

	Description of serving	Weight	Calorie Content per serving
Pineapple, tinned	11 cubes	150g (5¼oz)	116
Raisins, sultanas	2 handfuls	35g (1¼oz)	87
Satsuma	1 satsuma	100g (3½oz)	26
Strawberries	10 strawberries	85g (3oz)	26
Tangerine	1 tangerine	100g (3½oz)	23
Watermelon	1 slice	320g (11¼oz)	35

PROTEIN FOODS

Meat and Poultry

	Description of serving	Weight	Calorie Content per serving
Beef, roast	2 thick slices, lean	85g (3oz)	133
Beef, mince	5 tablespoons, stewed with onion	165g (5¾oz)	317
Beef, mince, lean	5 tablespoons, stewed with onion	165g (5¾oz)	216
Beefburgers	2 burgers, fried	90g (3oz)	238
Pork, roast	2 thick slices, lean	85g (3oz)	157
Pork chop	1 chop, grilled, lean	135g (4¾oz)	180
Gammon	1 steak	120g (4¼oz)	206
Bacon rasher	3 rashers, lean and fat, grilled	45g (1½oz)	182
Sausages, pork	2 sausages, grilled	90g (3oz)	286
Sausages, pork, low-fat	2 sausages, grilled	90g (3oz)	206
Sausage roll	1 sausage roll, flaky pastry	65g (2¼oz)	311
Ham	2 slices	55g (2oz)	66
Salami	5 slices	55g (2oz)	270
Lamb, roast	2 thick slices, lean	85g (3oz)	162
Lamb chops, lean and fat	2 chops, lean and fat, grilled	160g (5½oz)	443
Lamb chops, lean	2 chops, lean and fat, grilled	160g (5½oz)	195
Kidney, lamb's	2 kidneys, fried	75g (2¾oz)	116

	Description of serving	Weight		Calorie Content per serving
Chicken, roast	2 thick slices, breast	85g	(3oz)	121
Chicken, roast with skin	2 thick slices, breast	85g	(3oz)	184
Fish				
Cod steaks, grilled	2 steaks, grilled	130g	(4½oz)	124
Cod in batter, fried	1 piece, fried	85g	(3oz)	169
Plaice, steamed	2 small fillets	120g	(4¼oz)	112
Plaice in crumbs, fried	1 fillet, fried	105g	(3¾oz)	239
Haddock	2 fillets, steamed	130g	(4½oz)	127
Kipper	2 fillets, baked	130g	(4½oz)	267
Pilchards (in tomato sauce)	¼ large can	105g	(3¾oz)	132
Salmon, red	½ small can	115g	(4¼oz)	178
Sardines (in oil)	¾ can, drained	70g	(2½oz)	152
Tuna (in oil)	½ small can, drained	95g	(3¼oz)	180
Tuna (in brine)	½ small can	95g	(3¼oz)	95
Eggs and Egg Products				
Egg, boiled	1 size 2	60g	(2oz)	88
Egg, fried	1 size 2	60g	(2oz)	107
Quiche	1 slice	160g	(5½oz)	280
Pulses and Pulse Products				
Baked beans	½ large tin	200g	(7oz)	128
Black-eye beans	4 tablespoons, cooked	105g	(3¾oz)	122
Red kidney beans	4 tablespoons, cooked	105g	(3¾oz)	98
Soya beans	4 tablespoons, cooked	105g	(3¾oz)	148
Chick peas	4 tablespoons, cooked	105g	(3¾oz)	127
Lentils, green/brown	1 cup, cooked	150g	(5¼oz)	158
Lentils, red	1 cup, cooked	150g	(5¼oz)	150

	Description of serving	Weight		Calorie Content per serving
Tofu	piece 2"×3", steamed and fried	50g	(1¾oz)	130
Hummous	2 tablespoons	65g	(2¼oz)	120

Nuts and Seeds

Almonds	20 kernels	20g	(¾oz)	113
Brazil nuts	9 kernels	30g	(1oz)	186
Cashew nuts	20 kernels	40g	(1½oz)	224
Hazelnuts	30 whole nuts	25g	(1oz)	98
Peanuts	32 whole nuts	30g	(1oz)	171
Peanut butter	medium layer on slice, large loaf	7g		44
Sesame seeds	sprinkling	15g	(½oz)	88
Sunflower seeds	¼ cup	30g	(1oz)	174
Walnuts	9 halves	25g	(1oz)	131

MILKS AND DAIRY PRODUCTS

Milk, whole	⅓ pint	195g	(7oz)	129
Milk, semi-skimmed	⅓ pint	195g	(7oz)	90
Milk, skimmed	⅓ pint	195g	(7oz)	64
Soya milk	⅓ pint	195g	(7oz)	62
Goat's milk	⅓ pint	195g	(7oz)	117
Cheddar cheese	1 slice	40g	(1½oz)	165
Cheddar cheese, low-fat	1 slice	40g	(1½oz)	104
Edam cheese	1 slice	40g	(1½oz)	133
Full fat soft cheese	spread on two crispbreads	40g	(1½oz)	125
Cottage cheese	1 small carton	150g	(5¼oz)	117
Pizza	1 slice	160g	(5½oz)	376
Cheese sauce	made with whole milk	80g	(2¾oz)	158

	Description of serving	Weight	Calorie Content per serving
Cheese sauce	made with skimmed milk	80g (2¾oz)	134
Double cream	on pudding	35g (1¼oz)	157
Single cream	on pudding	35g (1¼oz)	69
Yoghurt, Greek, cow's milk	1 small carton	150g (5¼oz)	173
Yoghurt, low-fat, fruit	1 small carton	150g (5¼oz)	135
Fromage frais	1 small pot	45g (1½oz)	51
Ice cream, dairy	1 scoop	75g (2¾oz)	146
Custard, whole milk	3 tablespoons	75g (2¾oz)	88
Rice pudding, whole milk	3 tablespoons	85g (3oz)	110
Cheesecake	1 slice	100g (3½oz)	242
Milk chocolate	1 bar	50g (1¾oz)	265

FATS AND OILS

	Description of serving	Weight	Calorie Content per serving
Butter	medium layer on slice, large loaf	8g	59
Dairy fat spread	medium layer on slice, large loaf	8g	53
Low-fat spread	medium layer on slice, large loaf	8g	31
Very low-fat spread	medium layer on slice, large loaf	8g	22
Margarine, soft	medium layer on slice, large loaf	8g	59
Margarine, polyunsaturated	medium layer on slice, large loaf	8g	59
Ghee	1 dessertspoon	10g	29
Vegetable oils	1 dessertspoon	10g	26

	Description of serving	Weight		Calorie Content per serving
SUGARY FOODS				
Biscuits				
Chocolate digestive	2 biscuits	30g	(1oz)	148
Digestives	2 biscuits	30g	(1oz)	141
Custard creams	2 biscuits	25g	(1oz)	128
Rich tea	2 biscuits	15g	(½oz)	69
Cakes and Puddings				
Currant bun	1 bun	50g	(1¾oz)	148
Jam doughnut	1 doughnut	70g	(2½oz)	235
Fruit cake	1 slice	60g	(2oz)	215
Chocolate éclair	1 éclair	40g	(1½oz)	149
Sponge cake, jam filled	1 slice	35g	(1¼oz)	106
Fruit crumble	1 slice	120g	(4¼oz)	235
Lemon meringue pie	1 slice	95g	(3¼oz)	303
Trifle, dairy cream	1 serving	175g	(6¼oz)	291
Spreads and pickles				
Jam	medium layer on slice, large loaf	10g		29
Honey	medium layer on slice, large loaf	10g		26
Sweet pickle	1 tablespoon	35g	(1¼oz)	47
SOFT DRINKS				
Cola	1 glass	200g	(7oz)	78
Lemonade	1 glass	200g	(7oz)	42
Orange juice	1 glass, unsweetened	200g	(7oz)	66
Orange squash	to make up ⅓ pint glass	45g	(1½oz)	48

	Description of serving	Weight	Calorie Content per serving
Ribena	to make up ⅓ pint glass	45g (1½oz)	103

Estimated Average Requirement for Calories per day

Pre-pregnancy and Pregnancy (0–6 months)	= 1940 calories
Pregnancy (6–9 months)	= 2140 calories
Breastfeeding	= 2640 calories on average

(see pages 52 to 58 for more information)

TABLE 2
FIBRE CONTENT OF A SELECTION OF FOODS

	Description of serving	Weight	Fibre Content per serving
——————— STARCHY FOODS ———————			
All Bran	7 tablespoons	45g (1½oz)	13.5g
Muesli, no added sugar	6 tablespoons	95g (3¼oz)	10.5g
Bran Flakes	7 tablespoons	45g (1½oz)	8.0g
Pasta, wholemeal	6 tablespoons, cooked	150g (5¼oz)	6.0g
Pitta bread, wholemeal	1 pitta bread	65g (2¼oz)	6.0g
Bread, wholemeal	2 slices, large loaf	75g (2¾oz)	5.0g
Chapati	1 (made without fat)	70g (2½oz)	4.5g
Yam	⅙ average yam, boiled	130g (4½oz)	4.5g
Naan	1 naan	170g (6oz)	3.5g
Potato, jacket	1 large potato (with skin)	140g (5oz)	3.0g
Sweet potato	2 medium, boiled	150g (5¼oz)	3.0g

	Description of serving	Weight	Fibre Content per serving
Rice, brown	4 tablespoons, cooked	165g (5¾oz)	2.5g
Pitta bread, white	1 pitta bread	65g (2¼oz)	2.5g
Pasta, white	6 tablespoons, cooked	150g (5¼oz)	2.5g
Bread, white – high fibre	2 slices, large loaf	75g (2¾oz)	2.5g
Oven chips	4 tablespoons	120g (4¼oz)	2.5g
Potatoes, boiled	4 tablespoons	150g (5¼oz)	2.0g
Bread, white	2 slices, large loaf	75g (2¾oz)	1.5g
Rice, white	4 tablespoons, cooked	165g (5¾oz)	1.5g
Corn Flakes	6 tablespoons	35g (1¼oz)	1.5g

VEGETABLES

Peas, frozen	2½ tablespoons, boiled	75g (2¾oz)	8.0g
Spinach	2½ tablespoons, boiled	130g (4½oz)	7.5g
Leeks	1 small leek, boiled	125g (4½oz)	4.5g
Broccoli	2 spears, boiled	95g (3¼oz)	3.5g
Sweetcorn, tinned	2½ tablespoons	70g (2½oz)	3.5g
Brussels sprouts	11 sprouts, boiled	115g (4oz)	3.0g
Parsnips	2½ tablespoons, boiled	110g (4oz)	2.5g
Spring greens	3 tablespoons, boiled	75g (2¾oz)	2.0g
Beansprouts	1 cup	85g (3oz)	2.0g
Carrots	2½ tablespoons, boiled	65g (2¼oz)	2.0g
Tomatoes	2 medium sized (raw)	150g (5¼oz)	2.0g
Cauliflower	10 florets, boiled	100g (3½oz)	1.5g

FRUIT

Apricots, dried	8 apricots	50g (1¾oz)	11.0g
Figs, dried	4 figs	60g (2oz)	10.0g
Blackberries, raspberries	15 berries	75g (2¾oz)	5.0g
Prunes	8 prunes	40g (1½oz)	5.0g
Orange	1 large orange	245g (8½oz)	3.5g

	Description of serving	Weight	Fibre Content per serving
Banana	1 banana	135g (4¾oz)	2.5g
Raisins, sultanas	2 handfuls	35g (1¼oz)	2.0g
Apple	1 apple	120g (4¼oz)	1.5g

PROTEIN FOODS

Baked beans	½ large tin	200g (7oz)	13.0g
Beans, various	4 tablespoons, cooked	105g (3¾oz)	7.0g
Lentils, green/brown	1 cup, cooked	150g (5¼oz)	6.0g
Chick peas	4 tablespoons, cooked	105g (3¾oz)	4.5g
Lentils, red	1 cup, cooked	150g (5¼oz)	3.0g
Nuts, seeds	½ cup	30g (1oz)	2.0g

Recommended Nutrient Intake for Fibre per day

Pre-pregnancy = ⎫
Pregnancy = ⎬ 18g
Breastfeeding = ⎭

TABLE 3
PROPORTION OF FAT IN A SELECTION OF FOODS

	% Total fat	% Saturated fat	% Mono-unsaturated fat	% Poly-unsaturated fat
STARCHY FOODS				
Bread, crackers etc.				
Bread	2	<1	<1	<1

	% Total fat	% Saturated fat	% Mono-unsaturated fat	% Poly-unsaturated fat
Naan	13	N	N	N
Chapati	13	N	N	N
Chapati, non-fat	1			
Pitta bread	1			
Rye crispbread	2	<1	<1	1
Cream crackers	16	N	N	N
Scone, plain	15	5	6	4
Pasta, rice, potatoes				
Pasta	1			
Rice	1			
Potato (baked/boiled)	less than 1			
Potatoes (roast)	5	will depend on type of oil used		
Chips, fried in blended oil	12	1	6	5
Chips, fried in vegetable oil	12	4	5	3
Chips, fried in dripping	12	7	5	<1
Oven chips	4	2	2	<1
Sweet potato (boiled)	less than 1			
Yam (boiled)	less than 1			
Crisps	38	9	12	10
Crisps, low-fat	22	6	8	7
Breakfast cereals				
All Bran	3	<1	<1	2
Bran Flakes	2	<1	<1	1
Muesli, no added sugar	8	2	4	2
Corn Flakes	1			
Rice Krispies	1			

	% Total fat	% Saturated fat	% Mono-unsaturated fat	% Poly-unsaturated fat
VEGETABLES				
1% or less, except the following				
Avocado pear	20	3	9	2
Olives	11	2	6	1
Mushrooms, fried	16			
Okra, fried	26	will depend on type of oil used		
Onions, fried	11			
FRUIT				
less than 1%				
PROTEIN FOODS				
Meat and Poultry				
Beef, roast, lean	4	1	2	<1
Beef, mince (stewed)	15	7	7	<1
Beef, mince, lean (stewed)	7	2	3	1
Beefburgers, fried	17	8	8	<1
Pork, roast, lean	7	2	3	1
Pork chop, lean only, grilled	11	4	4	2
Gammon, lean, grilled	5	2	2	<1
Bacon rasher, lean and fat, grilled	35	14	16	4
Sausages, pork, grilled	25	10	11	3
Sausages, pork, low-fat, grilled	14	5	6	2
Sausage roll, flaky pastry	36	13	16	5
Ham	5	2	2	1
Salami	45	N	N	N

	% Total fat	% Saturated fat	% Mono-unsaturated fat	% Poly-unsaturated fat
Lamb, roast, lean	18	9	7	1
Lamb chops, lean and fat, grilled	29	14	11	1
Lamb chops, lean	12	6	5	<1
Kidney, lamb's	6	2	2	1
Chicken, roast, meat only	5	2	2	1
Chicken, roast with skin	14	4	7	3
Fish				
Cod steaks, grilled	1			
Cod in batter, fried	10	1	5	4
Plaice, steamed	2	<1	<1	<1
Plaice in crumbs, fried	14	1	5	6
Haddock, steamed	1			
Kipper, baked	11	2	6	3
Pilchards (in tomato sauce)	5	1	2	2
Salmon, red, canned	8	2	4	2
Sardines (in oil), drained	14	3	5	5
Tuna (in oil), drained	9	1	2	5
Tuna (in brine)	1			
Eggs and Egg Products				
Egg, boiled	11	3	5	1
Egg, fried	14	4	6	2
Quiche	22	10	8	2
Pulses and Pulse Products				
Baked beans, tinned	less than 1			
Black-eye beans, boiled	less than 1			

	% Total fat	% Saturated fat	% Mono- unsaturated fat	% Poly- unsaturated fat
Red kidney beans, boiled	less than 1			
Soya beans, boiled	7	1	1	4
Chick peas, boiled	2	<1	<1	1
Lentils, green/brown, boiled	less than 1			
Lentils, red, boiled	less than 1			
Tofu, steamed and fried	18	N	N	N
Hummous	13	N	N	N
Nuts and Seeds				
Almonds	56	5	34	14
Brazil nuts	68	16	26	23
Cashew nuts	51	10	29	9
Chestnuts	3	<1	1	1
Coconut	69	59	4	2
Hazelnuts	64	5	50	6
Pcanuts	46	8	21	14
Peanut butter	54	12	21	18
Sesame seeds	58	8	22	26
Sunflower seeds	48	5	10	31
Walnuts	69	6	12	48

——————— **MILKS AND DAIRY PRODUCTS** ———————

Milk, whole	4	2	1	<1
Milk, semi-skimmed	2	1	<1	<1
Milk, skimmed	less than 1			
Soya milk	2	<1	<1	1
Goat's milk	4	2	1	<1
Cheddar cheese	34	22	9	1

	% Total fat	% Saturated fat	% Mono-unsaturated fat	% Poly-unsaturated fat
Cheddar cheese, low-fat	15	9	4	<1
Edam cheese	25	16	7	1
Full fat soft cheese	31	19	9	1
Cottage cheese, low-fat	1			
Pizza	11	4	4	2
Cheese sauce, whole milk	15	8	5	2
Cheese sauce, semi-skimmed milk	12	6	4	2
Double cream	48	30	14	1
Single cream	19	12	6	<1
Condensed milk	10	6	3	<1
Evaporated milk	9	6	3	<1
Yoghurt, Greek, cow's milk	9	5	3	<1
Yoghurt, low-fat, fruit	1			
Fromage frais, fruit	6	4	2	<1
Ice cream, dairy	10	6	3	<1
Custard, whole milk	5	3	1	<1
Rice pudding, tinned	3	2	1	<1
Cheesecake	11	6	4	<1
Milk chocolate	30	18	10	2

FATS AND OILS

	% Total fat	% Saturated fat	% Mono-unsaturated fat	% Poly-unsaturated fat
Butter	82	54	20	3
Dairy fat spread	73	28	30	11
Low-fat spread	41	11	18	10
Very low-fat spread	25	7	14	3
Margarine, soft (animal and vegetable fat)	82	27	37	14

	% Total fat	% Saturated fat	% Mono-unsaturated fat	% Poly-unsaturated fat
Margarine, polyunsaturated	82	16	21	41
Ghee, butter	100	66	24	3
Ghee, palm oil	100	47	35	9
Dripping, beef	100	55	37	3
Lard	100	41	44	10
Coconut oil	100	85	7	2
Corn oil	100	13	25	58
Olive oil	100	14	70	11
Palm oil	100	45	42	8
Peanut oil	100	19	48	29
Safflower oil	100	10	13	72
Sesame oil	100	14	37	44
Soya oil	100	15	23	57
Sunflower oil	100	12	20	63
Vegetable oil*	100	10	36	48

SUGARY FOODS

Biscuits

Chocolate digestive	24	12	9	2
Digestives	21	9	10	2
Custard creams	26	15	8	2
Rich tea	17	8	6	2

Cakes and Puddings

Currant bun	8	N	N	N
Jam doughnut	15	4	5	4
Fruit cake	13	6	5	1
Chocolate éclair	31	16	10	2
Sponge cake, jam filled	5	2	2	1
Fruit crumble	7	2	2	2

	% Total fat	% Saturated fat	% Mono-unsaturated fat	% Poly-unsaturated fat
Lemon meringue pie	14	5	6	3
Trifle, dairy cream	9	5	3	<1

* The proportion of saturated fat, monounsaturated fat and polyunsaturated fat will depend on the blend of oils used.

N = figures not available

The proportion of the different types of fat has not been given when the fat content of the food is 1% or less.

TABLE 4

PROTEIN CONTENT OF A SELECTION OF FOODS

	Description of serving	Weight	Protein Content per serving
— STARCHY FOODS —			
Naan	1 naan	170g (6oz)	15g
Muesli, no added sugar	6 tablespoons	95g (3¼oz)	10g
Pasta, wholemeal	6 tablespoons, cooked	150g (5¼oz)	7g
All Bran	7 tablespoons	45g (1½oz)	7g
Bread	2 slices, large loaf	75g (2¾oz)	6g
Pitta bread	1 pitta bread	65g (2¼oz)	6g
Chapati	1 (made without fat)	70g (2½oz)	5g
Pasta, white	6 tablespoons, cooked	150g (5¼oz)	5g
Bran Flakes	7 tablespoons	45g (1½oz)	5g
Potatoes, jacket	1 large potato (with skin)	140g (5oz)	4g

	Description of serving	Weight	Protein Content per serving
Oven chips	4 tablespoons	120g (4¼oz)	4g
Rice (brown/white)	4 tablespoons, cooked	165g (5¾oz)	4g
Corn Flakes	6 tablespoons	35g (1¼oz)	3g
Rice Krispies	9 tablespoons	35g (1¼oz)	2g
Sweet potato	2 medium, boiled	150g (1¼oz)	2g
Potatoes, boiled	4 tablespoons	150g (5¼oz)	2g

VEGETABLES

Spinach	2½ tablespoons, boiled	130g (4½oz)	6g
Peas, frozen	2½ tablespoons, boiled	75g (2¾oz)	4g
Avocado pear	½ pear	130g (4¼oz)	4g
Broccoli	2 spears, boiled	95g (3¼oz)	3g
Beansprouts	1 cup	80g (2¾oz)	3g
Okra	2½ tablespoons, stir-fried	70g (2½oz)	3g
Sweetcorn, tinned	2½ tablespoons	70g (2½oz)	2g

FRUIT

Apricots, dried	8 apricots	50g (1¾oz)	2g
Figs, dried	4 figs	60g (2oz)	2g

PROTEIN FOODS

White fish	2 steaks	130g (4½oz)	27g
Red meat	2 thick slices, lean	85g (3oz)	25g
Oily fish	2 fillets	110g (4oz)	24g
Poultry	2 thick slices, breast	85g (3oz)	23g
Soya beans	4 tablespoons, cooked	105g (3¾oz)	14g
Lentils	1 cup, cooked	150g (5¼oz)	13g
Tofu	piece 2″ × 3″ steamed and fried	50g (1¾oz)	12g
Baked beans	½ large tin	200g (7oz)	10g

	Description of serving	Weight	Protein Content per serving
Chick peas	4 tablespoons, cooked	105g (3¾oz)	9g
Red kidney beans	4 tablespoons, cooked	105g (3¾oz)	9g
Black-eye beans	4 tablespoons, cooked	105g (3¾oz)	9g
Egg	1 size 2	60g (2oz)	7g
Peanuts	32 whole nuts	30g (1oz)	7g
Sesame seeds	sprinkling	15g (½oz)	4g
Hazelnuts	30 whole nuts	25g (1oz)	2g

MILKS AND DAIRY FOODS

	Description of serving	Weight	Protein Content per serving
Cottage cheese	1 small carton	150g (5¼oz)	19g
Cheese, Cheddar-type	1 slice	40g (1½oz)	10g
Milk (whole/skimmed)	⅓ pint	195g (7oz)	6g
Yoghurt, low-fat	1 small carton	150g (5¼oz)	6g

Recommended Nutrient Intake for Protein per day

Pre-pregnancy	= 45 gms
Pregnancy	= 51 gms
Breastfeeding (0–4 months)	= 56 gms
(4+ months)	= 53 gms

TABLE 5
VITAMIN A CONTENT OF A SELECTION OF FOODS

	Description of serving	Weight	Vitamin A Content per serving
STARCHY FOODS			
Sweet potato	2 medium, boiled	150g (5¼oz)	1000mcg
Naan	1 naan	170g (6oz)	165mcg
VEGETABLES			
Carrots	2½ tablespoons, boiled	65g (2¼oz)	1300mcg
Spinach	2½ tablespoons, boiled	130g (4½oz)	1300mcg
Spring greens	3 tablespoons, boiled	75g (2¾oz)	500mcg
Broccoli	2 spears, boiled	95g (3¼oz)	400mcg
Tomatoes	2 medium sized (raw)	150g (5¼oz)	150mcg
Watercress	¼ bunch	15g (½oz)	75mcg
Green beans	30 beans, boiled	105g (3¾oz)	70mcg
Lettuce	2–4 leaves	30g (1oz)	50mcg
FRUIT			
Mango	1 mango	315g (11oz)	370mcg
Melon, cantaloupe	¼ melon	180g (6¼oz)	350mcg
Apricots, dried	8 apricots	50g (1¾oz)	300mcg
Apricots, fresh	3 apricots	110g (4oz)	250mcg
Peach, nectarine	1 fruit	120g (4¼oz)	85mcg
Fig, fresh	1 fig	85g (3oz)	70mcg
PROTEIN FOODS			
*Liver, lamb's	2 slices, fried	90g (3oz)	18550mcg
Kidney, lamb's	2 kidneys, fried	75g (2¾oz)	120mcg
Egg	1 size 2	60g (2oz)	115mcg

	Description of serving	Weight	Vitamin A Content per serving
Salmon, red	½ small can	115g (4oz)	105mcg
Kipper	2 fillets, baked	130g (4½oz)	65mcg

MILKS AND DAIRY FOODS

Greek yoghurt, cow's milk	1 small carton	150g (5¼oz)	180mcg
Cheese, Cheddar-type	1 slice	40g (1½oz)	145mcg
Milk, whole	⅓ pint	195g (7oz)	110mcg
Milk, semi-skimmed	⅓ pint	195g (7oz)	45mcg

FATS AND OILS

Cod liver oil	1 teaspoon	5g	900mcg
Low-fat spread	medium layer on slice, large loaf	8g	85mcg
Ghee butter	1 dessertspoon	10g	75mcg
Butter, margarine	medium layer on slice, large loaf	8g	70mcg

* Liver and liver products should not be eaten in pregnancy due to the very high Vitamin A (retinol form) content.

Recommended Nutrient Intake for Vitamin A per day

Pre-pregnancy = 600mcg
Pregnancy   = 700mcg
Breastfeeding = 950mcg

TABLE 6
VITAMIN D CONTENT OF A SELECTION OF FOODS

	Description of serving	Weight	Vitamin D Content per serving
PROTEIN FOODS			
Herring	2 fillets, grilled	100g (3½oz)	25mcg
Salmon	½ small can	115g (4oz)	14mcg
Pilchards	¼ large can	105g (3¾oz)	8.5mcg
Tuna in oil	½ small can	95g (3¼oz)	5.5mcg
Egg	1 size 2	60g (2oz)	1.0mcg
MILKS AND DAIRY FOODS			
Condensed milk	3 tablespoons	45g (1½oz)	2.5mcg
Evaporated milk	2 tablespoons	30g (1oz)	1.2mcg
Milk, whole	½ pint	290g (10¼oz)	0.1mcg
FATS AND OILS			
Margarine	medium layer on slice, large loaf	8g	0,6mcg
Low-fat spread	medium layer on slice, large loaf	8g	0.6mcg
Ghee butter	1 dessertspoon	10g	0.2mcg
Ghee, vegetable/palm oil	1 dessertspoon	10g	NONE

Recommended Nutrient Intake for Vitamin D per day

Pre-pregnancy = No dietary requirement if skin exposed to sunlight
Pregnancy   = $\Big\}$ 10mcg
Breastfeeding =

TABLE 7
THIAMIN CONTENT OF A SELECTION OF FOODS

	Description of serving	Weight	Thiamin Content per serving
STARCHY FOODS			
All Bran	7 tablespoons	45g (1½oz	0.45mg
Bran Flakes	7 tablespoons	45g (1½oz)	0.45mg
Muesli, no added sugar	6 tablespoons	95g (3¼oz)	0.28mg
Corn Flakes	6 tablespoons	35g (1¼oz)	0.35mg
Rice Crispies	9 tablespoons	35g (1¼oz)	0.35mg
Pasta, wholemeal	6 tablespoons, cooked	150g (5¼oz)	0.32mg
Naan	1 naan	170g (6oz)	0.32mg
Bread, wholemeal	2 slices, large loaf	75g (2¾oz)	0.24mg
Rice, brown	4 tablespoons, cooked	165g (5¾oz)	0.23mg
Bread, white	2 slices, large loaf	75g (2¾oz)	0.16mg
Chapati, non-fat	1 (made without fat)	70g (2½oz)	0.16mg
Pitta bread	1 pitta bread	65g (2¼oz)	0.16mg
Potato, jacket	1 large potato (with skin)	140g (5oz)	0.14mg
Oven chips	4 tablespoons	120g (4¼oz)	0.13mg
Sweet potato	2 medium, boiled	150g (5¼oz)	0.12mg
Yam	⅙ average yam, boiled	130g (4½oz)	0.07mg
Pasta, white	6 tablespoons, cooked	150g (5¼oz)	0.02mg
Rice, white	4 tablespoons, cooked	165g (5¾oz)	0.02mg
VEGETABLES			
Peas, frozen	2½ tablespoons, boiled	75g (2¾oz)	0.18mg
Leeks	1 small leek, boiled	125g (4½oz)	0.09mg
Spinach	2½ tablespoons, boiled	130g (4½oz)	0.09mg
Avocado pear	½ pear	130g (4½oz)	0.09mg
Tomatoes	2 medium sized (raw)	150g (5¼oz)	0.08mg
Broad beans	1 heaped tablespoon, boiled	75g (2¾oz)	0.08mg

	Description of serving	Weight	Thiamin Content per serving
Parsnips	2½ tablespoons, boiled	110g (4oz)	0.08mg
Brussels sprouts	11 sprouts, boiled	115g (4oz)	0.07mg
Cauliflower	10 florets, boiled	100g (3½oz)	0.06mg
Broccoli	2 spears, boiled	95g (3¼oz)	0.06mg

FRUIT

Orange	1 large orange	245g (8½oz)	0.20mg
Pineapple (fresh)	1 slice	125g (4½oz)	0.10mg
Figs, dried	4 figs	60g (2oz)	0.06mg
Apple	1 apple	120g (4¼oz)	0.04mg
Raisins, sultanas	2 handfuls	35g (1¼oz)	0.04mg

PROTEIN FOODS

Gammon	1 steak	120g (4¼oz)	1.20mg
Pork chop	1 chop, grilled, lean	135g (4¾oz)	0.70mg
Sunflower seeds	¼ cup	30g (1oz)	0.48mg
Kidney, lamb's	2 kidneys, fried	75g (2¾oz)	0.42mg
Plaice	2 fillets, steamed	125g (4½oz)	0.36mg
Brazil nuts	9 kernels	30g (1oz)	0.30mg
Peanuts	32 while nuts	30g (1oz)	0.30mg
Salmon steak	1 steak	135g (4¾oz)	0.22mg
Lentils, green/brown	1 cup, cooked	150g (5¼oz)	0.20mg
Pulses, various	4 tablespoons, cooked	105g (3¾oz)	0.10–0.20mg
Lentils, red	1 cup, cooked	150g (5¼oz)	0.17mg
Baked beans	½ large tin	200g (7oz)	0.14mg
Egg	1 size 2	60g (2oz)	0.04mg

MILKS

Soya milk	⅓ pint	195g (7oz)	0.12mg
Milk (whole/skimmed)	⅓ pint	195g (7oz)	0.08mg

	Description of serving	Weight	Thiamin Content per serving
MISCELLANEOUS			
Bovril	1 teaspoon	5g	0.46mg
Marmite	1 teaspoon	5g	0.16mg

Recommended Nutrient Intake for Thiamin per day

Pre-pregnancy = $\left.\right\}$ 0.8mg
Pregnancy =
Breastfeeding = 1.0mg

TABLE 8
RIBOFLAVIN CONTENT OF A SELECTION OF FOODS

	Description of serving	Weight	Riboflavin Content per serving
STARCHY FOODS			
All Bran	7 tablespoons	45g (1½oz)	0.68mg
Bran Flakes	7 tablespoons	45g (1½oz)	0.68mg
Corn Flakes	6 tablespoons	35g (1¼oz)	0.53mg
Rice Krispies	9 tablespoons	35g (1¼oz)	0.53mg
Muesli, no added sugar	6 tablespoons	95g (3¼oz)	0.28mg
Naan	1 naan	170g (6oz)	0.17mg
Bread, wholemeal	2 slices, large loaf	75g (2¾oz)	0.06mg
Potato, jacket	1 large potato (with skin)	140g (5oz)	0.06mg
Bread, white	2 slices, large loaf	75g (2¾oz)	0.05mg

APPENDIX TWO: NUTRIENT CONTENTS AND SERVING SIZE

	Description of serving	Weight	Riboflavin Content per serving
VEGETABLES			
Mushrooms	10 button mushrooms, fried	55g (2oz)	0.20mg
Broccoli	2 spears, boiled	95g (3¼oz)	0.20mg
Spinach	2½ tablespoons, boiled	130g (4½oz)	0.20mg
Spring greens	3 tablespoons, boiled	75g (2¾oz)	0.15mg
Beansprouts	1 cup	85g (3oz)	0.11mg
PROTEIN FOODS			
Kidney, lamb's	2 kidneys, fried	75g (2¾oz)	1.73mg
Pilchards	¼ large can	105g (3¾oz)	0.30mg
Red meat	2 thick slices, lean	85g (3oz)	0.28mg
Sardines in oil	¾ can, drained	70g (2½oz)	0.25mg
Egg	1 size 2	60g (2oz)	0.21mg
Chicken	2 thick slices, breast	85g (3oz)	0.20mg
Almonds	20 kernels	20g (¾oz)	0.18mg
Plaice	2 fillets, steamed	125g (4½oz)	0.13mg
Lentils, green/brown	1 cup, cooked	150g (5¼oz)	0.12mg
Baked beans	½ large tin	200g (7oz)	0.10mg
Cashew nuts	20 kernels	40g (1½oz)	0.10mg
Pulses, various	4 tablespoons, cooked	105g (3¾oz)	0.05–0.1mg
Lentils, red	1 cup, cooked	150g (5¼oz)	0.06mg
MILK AND DAIRY FOODS			
Greek yoghurt, cow's milk	1 small carton	150g (5¼oz)	0.54mg
Soya milk	⅓ pint	195g (7oz)	0.53mg
Milk, whole/skimmed	⅓ pint	195g (7oz)	0.33mg
Yoghurt, low-fat	1 small carton	150g (5¼oz)	0.32mg
Cottage cheese	1 small carton	150g (5¼oz)	0.40mg

	Description of serving	Weight	Riboflavin Content per serving
Cheese, Cheddar-type, reduced-fat	1 slice	40g (1½oz)	0.21mg
Cheese, Cheddar-type	1 slice	40g (1½oz)	0.16mg

MISCELLANEOUS

	Description of serving	Weight	Riboflavin Content per serving
Marmite	1 teaspoon	5g	0.55mg
Bovril	1 teaspoon	5g	0.38mg

Recommended Nutrient Intake for Riboflavin per day

Pre-pregnancy = 1.1mg
Pregnancy = 1.4mg
Breastfeeding = 1.6mg

TABLE 9
NIACIN CONTENT OF A SELECTION OF FOODS

	Description of serving	Weight	Niacin Content per serving

STARCHY FOODS

	Description of serving	Weight	Niacin Content per serving
All Bran	7 tablespoons	45g (1½oz)	8.6mg
Bran Flakes	7 tablespoons	45g (1½oz)	8.3mg
Muesli, no added sugar	6 tablespoons	95g (3¼oz)	7.1mg
Rice Krispies	9 tablespoons	35g (1¼oz)	6.1mg
Corn Flakes	6 tablespoons	35g (1¼oz)	5.9mg
Naan	1 naan	170g (6oz)	5.1mg
Bread, wholemeal	2 slices, large loaf	75g (2¾oz)	4.1mg

	Description of serving	Weight	Niacin Content per serving
Pasta, wholemeal	6 tablespoons, cooked	150g (5¼oz)	3.5mg
Rice, brown	4 tablespoons, cooked	165g (5¾oz)	3.1mg
Bread, white	2 slices, large loaf	165g (5¾oz)	2.6mg
Oven chips	4 tablespoons	120g (4¼oz)	2.6mg
Potato, jacket	1 large potato (with skin)	140g (5oz)	2.5mg
Chapati, non-fat	1 (made without fat)	70g (2½oz)	2.4mg
Pasta, white	6 tablespoons, cooked	150g (5¼oz)	1.8mg
Sweet potato	2 medium, boiled	150g (5¼oz)	1.4mg
Rice, white	4 tablespoons, cooked	165g (5¾oz)	1.3mg

––––––––––––––– VEGETABLES –––––––––––––––

Broad beans	1 heaped tablespoon, boiled	75g (2¾oz)	2.8mg
Mushrooms	10 button mushrooms, fried	55g (2oz)	2.4mg
Spinach	2½ tablespoons, boiled	130g (4½oz)	2.3mg
Peas, frozen	2½ tablespoons, boiled	75g (2¾oz)	1.8mg
Avocado pear	½ pear	130g (4½oz)	1.6mg
Swede	3 tablespoons, boiled	120g (4¼oz)	1.2mg
Tomatoes	2 medium sized (raw)	150g (5¼oz)	1.2mg

––––––––––––––– FRUIT –––––––––––––––

Apricots, dried	8 apricots	50g (1¾oz)	1.9mg
Guavas, tinned	6 halves	175g (6¼oz)	1.8mg
Figs, dried	4 figs	60g (2oz)	1.3mg
Peach, nectarine	1 fruit	120g (4¼oz)	1.1mg

	Description of serving	Weight	Niacin Content per serving
PROTEIN FOODS			
Tuna (in oil)	½ small can, drained	95g (3¼oz)	16.3mg
Chicken	2 thick slices, breast	85g (3oz)	13.0mg
Salmon, red	½ small can	115g (4oz)	12.4mg
Pork	1 chop, grilled, lean	135g (4¾oz)	10.9mg
Beef	2 thick slices, lean	85g (3oz)	10.8mg
Cod	2 steaks, grilled	130g (4½oz)	7.5mg
Peanuts	32 whole nuts	30g (1oz)	6.4mg
Sunflower seeds	¼ cup	30g (1oz)	2.7mg
Lentils, green/brown	1 cup, cooked	150g (5¼oz)	2.7mg
Baked beans	½ large tin	200g (7oz)	2.6mg
Egg	1 size 2	60g (2oz)	2.3mg
Pulses, various	4 tablespoons, cooked	105g (3¾oz)	2.0–3.0mg
Tofu	piece 2″ × 3″, steamed and fried	50g (1¾oz)	2.0mg
Lentils, red	1 cup, cooked	150g (5¼oz)	2.0mg
Sesame seeds	sprinkling	15g (½oz)	1.9mg
MILKS AND DAIRY FOODS			
Cottage cheese	1 small carton	150g (5¼oz)	5.0mg
Cheese, cheddar-type, reduced-fat	1 slice	40g (1½oz)	3.0mg
Cheese, Cheddar-type	1 slice	40g (1½oz)	2.4mg
Greek yoghurt, cow's milk	1 small carton	150g (5¼oz)	2.4mg
Yoghurt, low-fat	1 small carton	150g (5¼oz)	1.7mg
Milk (whole/skimmed)	⅓ pint	195g (7oz)	1.7mg
Soya milk	⅓ pint	195g (7oz)	1.2mg

	Description of serving	Weight	Niacin Content per serving
MISCELLANEOUS			
Bovril	1 teaspoon	5g	4.3mg
Marmite	1 teaspoon	5g	3.4mg

Recommended Nutrient Intake for Niacin per day

Pre-pregnancy = ⎫
Pregnancy   = ⎬ 13.2mg
Breastfeeding = 15.5mg

TABLE 10
VITAMIN B6 CONTENT OF A SELECTION OF FOODS

	Description of serving	Weight	Vitamin B6 Content per serving
STARCHY FOODS			
Bran Flakes	7 tablespoons	45g (1½oz)	0.81mg
Potato, jacket	1 large potato (with skin)	140g (5oz)	0.76mg
Corn Flakes	6 tablespoons	35g (1¼oz)	0.63mg
Rice Krispies	9 tablespoons	35g (1¼oz)	0.63mg
All Bran	7 tablespoons	45g (1½oz)	0.59mg
Muesli, no added sugar	6 tablespoons	95g (3¼oz)	0.29mg
Naan	1 naan	170g (6oz)	0.22mg
Chapati, non-fat	1 (made without fat)	70g (2½oz)	0.13mg
Pasta, wholemeal	6 tablespoons, cooked	150g (5¼oz)	0.12mg

	Description of serving	Weight	Vitamin B6 Content per serving
Bread, wholemeal	2 slices, large loaf	75g (2¾oz)	0.09mg
Bread, white	2 slices, large loaf	75g (2¾oz)	0.04mg

VEGETABLES

Avocado pear	½ pear	130g (4½oz)	0.47mg
Tomatoes	2 medium sized (raw)	150g (5¼oz)	0.22mg
Red pepper	¼ pepper (raw)	45g (1½oz)	0.16mg
Cauliflower	10 florets, boiled	100g (3½oz)	0.15mg
Spring greens	3 tablespoons, boiled	75g (2¾oz)	0.14mg
Spinach	2½ tablespoons, boiled	130g (4½oz)	0.12mg
Broccoli	2 spears, boiled	95g (3¼oz)	0.10mg

FRUIT

Watermelon	1 slice	320g (11¼oz)	0.45mg
Mango	1 mango	315g (11oz)	0.28mg
Banana	1 banana	135g (4¾oz)	0.26mg
Orange	1 large orange	245g (8½oz)	0.25mg
Figs, dried	4 figs	60g (2oz)	0.14mg
Grapes, (white/black)	small bunch	140g (5oz)	0.14mg
Raisins, sultanas	2 handfuls	35g (1¼oz)	0.09mg

PROTEIN FOODS

Salmon, red	½ small can	115g (4oz)	0.52mg
Tuna (in oil)	½ small can, drained	95g (3¼oz)	0.48mg
Lentils, green/brown	1 cup, cooked	150g (5¼oz)	0.42mg
Pork	1 chop, grilled, lean	135g (4¾oz)	0.32mg
Chicken	2 thick slices, breast	85g (3oz)	0.30mg
Beef	2 thick slices, lean	85g (3oz)	0.28mg
Soya beans	4 tablespoons, cooked	105g (3¾oz)	0.24mg
Sunflower seeds	¼ cup	30g (1oz)	0.21mg
Peanuts	32 whole nuts	30g (1oz)	0.19mg

	Description of serving	Weight	Vitamin B6 Content per serving
Walnuts	9 halves	25g (1oz)	0.17mg
Lentils, red	1 cup, cooked	150g (5¼oz)	0.17mg
Hazelnuts	30 whole nuts	25g (1oz)	0.15mg
Chick peas	4 tablespoons, cooked	105g (3¾oz)	0.15mg
Red kidney beans	4 tablespoons, cooked	105g (3¾oz)	0.12mg
Sesame seeds	sprinkling	15g (½oz)	0.11mg

MILKS AND DAIRY FOODS

Soya milk	⅓ pint	195g (7oz)	0.14mg
Milk (whole/skimmed)	⅓ pint	195g (7oz)	0.12mg
Yoghurt, low-fat, fruit	1 small carton	150g (5¼oz)	0.12mg
Cottage cheese	1 small carton	150g (5¼oz)	0.12mg
Cheese, Cheddar-type	1 slice (full fat or fat reduced)	40g (1½oz)	0.04mg

Recommended Nutrient Intake for Vitamin B6 per day

Pre-pregnancy =
Pregnancy   =   } 0.96mg
Breastfeeding =

TABLE II
FOLATE CONTENT OF A SELECTION OF FOODS

	Description of serving	Weight	Folate Content per serving
STARCHY FOODS			
All Bran	7 tablespoons	45g (1½oz)	86mcg
Bran Flakes	7 tablespoons	45g (1½oz)	113mcg
Corn Flakes	6 tablespoons	35g (1¼oz)	88mcg
Rice Krispies	9 tablespoons	35g (1¼oz)	88mcg
Bread, white – high fibre	2 slices, large loaf	75g (2¾oz)	70mcg
Bread, granary	2 slices, large loaf	75g (2¾oz)	68mcg
Potato, jacket	1 large potato (with skin)	140g (5oz)	39mcg
Bread, wholemeal	2 slices, large loaf	75g (2¾oz)	29mcg
Oven chips	4 tablespoons	120g (4¼oz)	25mcg
Naan	1 naan	170g (6oz)	24mcg
Bread, white	2 slices, large loaf	75g (2¾oz)	22mcg
VEGETABLES			
Brussels sprouts	11 sprouts, boiled	115g (4oz)	127mcg
Spinach	2½ tablespoons, boiled	130g (4½oz)	117mcg
Broccoli	2 spears, boiled	95g (3¼oz)	61mcg
Green beans	30 beans, boiled	105g (3¾oz)	59mcg
Cauliflower	10 florets, boiled	100g (3½oz)	51mcg
Peas, frozen	2½ tablespoons, boiled	75g (2¾oz)	35mcg
Cabbage	3 tablespoons, boiled	75g (2¾oz)	22mcg
FRUIT			
Orange	1 large orange	245g (8½oz)	54mcg
Blackberries	15 blackberries	75g (2¾oz)	27mcg
Grapefruit	½ grapefruit	140g (5oz)	25mcg
Satsuma	1 satsuma	100g (3½oz)	23mcg

	Description of serving	Weight	Folate Content per serving
PROTEIN FOODS			
Black-eye beans	4 tablespoons, cooked	105g (3¾oz)	220mcg
Sunflower seeds	¼ cup	30g (1oz)	68mcg
Soya beans	4 tablespoons, cooked	105g (3¾oz)	59mcg
Chick peas	4 tablespoons, cooked	105g (3¾oz)	59mcg
Red kidney beans	4 tablespoons, cooked	105g (3¾oz)	44mcg
Peanuts	32 whole nuts	30g (1oz)	33mcg
Eggs	1 size 2	60g (2oz)	23mcg
MILKS AND DAIRY PRODUCTS			
Cottage chese	1 small carton	150g (5¼oz)	40mcg
Soya milk	⅓ pint	195g (7oz)	37mcg
Yoghurt, low-fat, fruit	1 small carton	150g (5¼oz)	24mcg
Cheese, Cheddar-type, reduced-fat	1 slice	40g (1½oz)	22mcg
Cheese, Cheddar-type	1 slice	40g (½oz)	13mcg
Milk (whole/skimmed)	⅓ pint	195g (7oz)	12mcg
MISCELLANEOUS			
Marmite	1 teaspoon	5g	50mcg
Bovril	1 teaspoon	5g	50mcg

Recommended Nutrient Intake for Folate per day

Pre-pregnancy = ⎫
Pregnancy   = ⎬ 300mcg + 400mcg supplement until 12th week of pregnancy
Breastfeeding = 260mcg

TABLE 12
VITAMIN B12 CONTENT OF A SELECTION OF FOODS

	Description of serving	Weight	Vitamin B12 Content per serving
STARCHY FOODS			
Bran Flakes	7 tablespoons	45g (1½oz)	0.8mcg
Corn Flakes	6 tablespoons	35g (1¼oz)	0.8mcg
Rice Krispies	9 tablespoons	35g (1¼oz)	0.8mcg
All Bran	7 tablespoons	45g (1½oz)	0.6mcg
PROTEIN FOODS			
Sardines (in oil)	¾ can, drained	70g (2½oz)	19.6mcg
Pilchards (in tomato sauce)	¼ large can	105g (3¾oz)	12.6mcg
Tuna (in oil)	½ small can, drained	95g (3¼oz)	4.6mcg
Textured vegetable protein		85g (3oz)	4.3mcg
Red meat	2 thick slices, lean, roasted	85g (3oz)	1.7mcg
Egg	1 size 2	60g (2oz)	0.7mcg
MILKS AND DAIRY FOODS			
Soya milk, fortified	⅓ pint	195g (7oz)	6.2mcg
Cottage cheese	1 small carton	150g (5¼oz)	1.0mcg
Milk (whole/skimmed)	⅓ pint	195g (7oz)	0.8mcg
Cheese, Cheddar-type	1 slice (full-fat or reduced-fat)	40g (1½oz)	0.4mcg

	Description of serving	Weight	Vitamin B12 Content per serving
MISCELLANEOUS			
Seaweed (Spirulina)		15g	7.5mcg
Vecon stock cube	1 cube	10g	1.3mcg
Marmite	1 teaspoon	5g	0.4mcg

Recommended Nutrient Intake for Vitamin B12 per day

Pre-pregnancy = ⎫
Pregnancy   = ⎬ 1.5mcg
Breastfeeding = 2.0mcg

TABLE 13
VITAMIN C CONTENT OF A SELECTION OF FOODS

	Description of serving	Weight	Vitamin C Content per serving
STARCHY FOODS			
Sweet potato	2 medium, boiled	150g (5¼oz)	23mg
Potato, jacket	1 large potato (with skin)	140g (5oz)	20mg
Oven chips	4 tablespoons	120g (4¼oz)	14mg
VEGETABLES			
Brussels sprouts	11 sprouts, boiled	115g (4oz)	46mg
Green pepper	¼ pepper (raw)	45g (1½oz)	45mg
Spinach	2½ tablespoons, boiled	130g (4½oz)	33mg

	Description of serving	Weight	Vitamin C Content per serving
Broccoli	2 spears, boiled	95g (3¼oz)	32mg
Tomatoes	2 medium sized (raw)	150g (5¼oz)	30mg
Spring greens	3 tablespoons, boiled	75g (2¾oz)	23mg
Cauliflower	10 florets, boiled	100g (3½oz)	20mg
Swede	3 tablespoons, boiled	120g (4¼oz)	20mg
Leeks	1 small leek, boiled	125g (4½oz)	19mg
Cabbage	3 tablespoons, boiled	75g (2½oz)	11mg
Green beans	30 beans, boiled	105g (3¾oz)	5mg
Lettuce	2–4 leaves	30g (1oz)	5mg

FRUIT

Guavas, tinned	6 halves	175g (6¼oz)	315mg
Orange	1 large orange	245g (8½oz)	93mg
Strawberries	10 strawberries	85g (3oz)	51mg
Mango	1 mango	315g (11oz)	56mg
Honeydew Melon	1 slice	190g (6¾oz)	29mg
Gooseberries	11 gooseberries	70g (2½oz)	28mg
Grapefruit	½ grapefruit	140g (5oz)	27mg
Tangerine	1 tangerine	100g (3½oz)	21mg
Pineapple, tinned	11 cubes	150g (5¼oz)	18mg
Blackberries	15 blackberries	80g (2¾oz)	16mg

MISCELLANEOUS

Orange juice	⅓ pint	195g (7oz)	68mg

Recommended Nutrient Intake for Vitamin C per day

Pre-pregnancy = 40mg
Pregnancy = 50mg
Breastfeeding = 70mg

TABLE 14
CALCIUM CONTENT OF A SELECTION OF FOODS

	Description of serving	Weight	Calcium Content per serving
STARCHY FOODS			
Naan	1 naan	170g (6oz)	273mg
Bread, white	2 slices, large loaf	75g (2¾oz)	83mg
Pitta bread, white	1 pitta bread	65g (2¼oz)	59mg
Bread, wholemeal	2 slices, large loaf	75g (2¾oz)	38mg
Chapati, non-fat	1 (made without fat)	70g (2½oz)	42mg
VEGETABLES			
Spinach	2½ tablespoons, boiled	130g (4½oz)	780mg
Leeks	1 small leek, boiled	125g (4½oz)	76mg
Broccoli	2 spears, boiled	95g (3¼oz)	72mg
Green beans	30 beans, boiled	105g (3¾oz)	59mg
Broad beans	1 heaped tablespoon, boiled	75g (2¾oz)	42mg
Cabbage	3 tablespoons, boiled	75g (2¾oz)	40mg
Parsnips	2½ tablespoons, boiled	110g (4oz)	40mg
FRUIT			
Figs, dried	4 figs	60g (2oz)	168mg
Orange	1 large orange	245g (8½oz)	76mg
Blackberries	15 blackberries	75g (2¾oz)	68mg
PROTEIN FOODS			
Tofu	piece 2″ × 3″, steamed and fried	50g (1¾oz)	740mg
Sardines (in oil)	¾ can, drained	70g (2½oz)	385mg

	Description of serving	Weight	Calcium Content per serving
Pilchards (in tomato sauce)	¼ large can	105g (3¾oz)	315mg
Baked beans	½ large tin	200g (7oz)	106mg
Sesame seeds	sprinkling	15g (½oz)	101mg
Soya beans	4 tablespoons, cooked	105g (3¾oz)	87mg
Kipper	2 fillets, baked	130g (4½oz)	85mg
Brazil nuts	9 kernels	30g (1oz)	54mg
Almonds	20 kernels	20g (¾oz)	50mg
Chick peas	4 tablespoons, cooked	105g (3¾oz)	48mg
Red kidney beans	4 tablespoons, cooked	105g (3¾oz)	39mg

MILKS AND DAIRY FOODS

Cheese, Cheddar-type, reduced-fat	1 slice	40g (1½oz)	336mg
Cheese, Cheddar-type	1 slice	40g (1½oz)	288mg
Soya milk, fortified	⅓ pint	195g (7oz)	273mg
Milk (whole/skimmed)	⅓ pint	195g (7oz)	230mg
Yoghurt, low-fat, fruit	1 small carton	150g (5¼oz)	225mg
Greek yoghurt, cow's milk	1 small carton	150g (5¼oz)	225mg
Goat's milk	⅓ pint	195g (7oz)	195mg
Cottage cheese	1 small carton	150g (5¼oz)	110mg
Fromage frais	1 small pot	45g (1½oz)	40mg

MISCELLANEOUS

Thyme	1 teaspoon	5g	95mg
Sage	1 teaspoon	5g	83mg
Garam masala	2 teaspoons	10g	76mg
Rosemary	1 teaspoon	5g	64mg
Curry powder	2 teaspoons	10g	64mg

Recommended Nutrient Intake for Calcium per day

Pre-pregnancy = 700mg
Pregnancy   = 800mg
Breastfeeding = 1250mg

TABLE 15

POTASSIUM CONTENT OF A SELECTION OF FOODS

	Description of serving	Weight	Potassium Content per serving
STARCHY FOODS			
Potato, jacket	1 large potato (with skin	140g (5oz)	882mg
Oven chips	4 tablespoons	120g (4¼oz)	636mg
Sweet potato	2 medium, boiled	150g (5¼oz)	450mg
All Bran	7 tablespoons	45g (1½oz)	450mg
Muesli, no added sugar	6 tablespoons	95g (3¼oz)	318mg
Naan	1 naan	170g (6oz)	306mg
Bran Flakes	7 tablespoons	45g (1½oz)	243mg
Bread, wholemeal	2 slices, large loaf	75g (2¾oz)	173mg
Chapati, non-fat	1 (made without fat)	70g (2½oz)	105mg
Bread, white	2 slices, large loaf	75g (2¾oz)	83mg
VEGETABLES			
Avocado pear	½ pear	130g (4½oz)	585mg
Parsnips	2½ tablespoons, boiled	110g (4oz)	385mg
Tomatoes	2 medium sized (raw)	150g (5¼oz)	376mg
Spinach	2½ tablespoons, boiled	130g (4½oz)	300mg
Mushrooms	10 button mushrooms	55g (2oz)	187mg
Broccoli	2 spears, boiled	95g (3¼oz)	162mg

	Description of serving	Weight	Potassium Content per serving
FRUIT			
Apricots, dried	8 apricots	50g (1¾oz)	690mg
Banana	1 banana	135g (4¾oz)	365mg
Watermelon	1 slice	190g (6¾oz)	320mg
Prunes	8 prunes	40g (1½oz)	304mg
Orange	1 large orange	245g (8½oz)	270mg
Apple	1 apple	120g (4¼oz)	144mg
PROTEIN FOODS			
Kipper	2 fillets, baked	130g (4½oz)	676mg
Lentils, green/brown	1 cup cooked	150g (5¼oz)	465mg
Cod	2 steaks, grilled	130g (4½oz)	456mg
Red kidney beans	4 tablespoons, cooked	105g (3¾oz)	441mg
Pilchards (in tomato sauce)	¼ large can	105g (3¾oz)	441mg
Black-eye beans	4 tablespoons, cooked	105g (3¾oz)	336mg
Lentils, red	1 cup, cooked	150g (5¼oz)	330mg
Red meat	2 thick slices, lean, roasted	85g (3oz)	300mg
Cashew nuts	20 kernels	40g (1½oz)	292mg
Chick peas	4 tablespoons, cooked	105g (3¾oz)	284mg
Chicken	2 thick slices, breast, roasted	85g (3oz)	281mg
Sunflower seeds	¼ cup	30g (1oz)	213mg
Peanuts	32 whole nuts	30g (1oz)	201mg
Hazelnuts	30 whole nuts	25g (1oz)	182mg
Almonds	20 kernels	20g (¾oz)	156mg

	Description of serving	Weight	Potassium Content per serving
MILKS AND DAIRY FOODS			
Yoghurt, low-fat, fruit	1 small carton	150g (5¼oz)	315mg
Milk, semi-skimmed	⅓ pint	195g (7oz)	293mg
Milk, whole	⅓ pint	195g (7oz)	273mg
Soya milk	⅓ pint	195g (7oz)	234mg

Recommended Nutrient Intake for Potassium per day

Pre-pregnancy = ⎫
Pregnancy = ⎬ 3500 mg
Breastfeeding = ⎭

TABLE 16

MAGNESIUM CONTENT OF A SELECTION OF FOODS

	Description of serving	Weight	Magnesium Content per serving
STARCHY FOODS			
All Bran	7 tablespoons	45g (1½oz)	167mg
Muesli, no added sugar	6 tablespoons	95g (3¼oz)	86mg
Rice, brown	4 tablespoons, cooked	165g (5¾oz)	71mg
Sweet potato	2 medium, boiled	150g (5¼oz)	68mg
Bran Flakes	7 tablespoons	45g (1½oz)	59mg
Bread, wholemeal	2 slices, large loaf	75g (2¾oz)	57mg
Naan	1 naan	170g (6oz)	48mg
Potato, jacket	1 large potato (with skin)	140g (5oz)	41mg

	Description of serving	Weight	Magnesium Content per serving
Oven chips	4 tablespoons	120g (4¼oz)	32mg
Chapati, non-fat	1 (made without fat)	70g (2½oz)	26mg
Bread, white – high fibre	2 slices, large loaf	75g (2¾oz)	23mg
Rice, white	4 tablespoons, cooked	165g (5¾oz)	18mg
Bread, white	2 slices, large loaf	75g (2¾oz)	15mg

VEGETABLES

Okra	2½ tablespoons, stir-fried	70g (2½oz)	77mg
Spinach	2½ tablespoons, boiled	130g (4½oz)	44mg
Parsnips	2½ tablespoons, boiled	110g (4oz)	25mg
Avocado pear	½ pear	130g (4½oz)	23mg
Peas, frozen	2½ tablespoons, boiled	75g (2¾oz)	22mg
Sweetcorn, tinned	2½ tablespoons	70g (2½oz)	16mg

PROTEIN FOODS

Brazil nuts	9 kernels	30g (1oz)	123mg
Sunflower seeds	¼ cup	30g (1oz)	117mg
Soya beans	4 tablespoons, cooked	105g (3¾oz)	66mg
Baked beans	½ large tin	200g (7oz)	62mg
Sesame seeds	sprinkling	15g (½oz)	56mg
Peanuts	32 whole nuts	30g (1oz)	54mg
Almonds	20 kernels	20g (¾oz)	52mg
Lentils, green/brown	1 cup, cooked	150g (5¼oz)	51mg
Red kidney beans	4 tablespoons, cooked	105g (3¾oz)	47mg
Pilchards (in tomato sauce)	¼ large can	105g (3¾oz)	41mg
Chick peas	4 tablespoons, cooked	105g (3¾oz)	39mg
Lentils, red	1 cup, cooked	150g (5¼oz)	39mg
Sardines (in oil)	¾ can, drained	70g (2½oz)	36mg
Cod	2 steaks, grilled	130g (4½oz)	34g

	Description of serving	Weight	Magnesium Content per serving
Tuna (in oil)	½ small can, drained	95g (3¼oz)	31mg
Red meat, poultry	2 thick slices, lean, roasted	85g (3oz)	22mg

MILKS AND DAIRY FOODS

Yoghurt, low-fat fruit	1 small carton	150g (5¼oz)	23mg
Milk (whole/skimmed)	⅓ pint	195g (7oz)	22mg

MISCELLANEOUS

Garam masala	2 teaspoons	10g	33mg
Curry powder	2 teaspoons	10g	28mg
Sage	1 teaspoon	5g	22mg

Recommended Nutrient Intake for Magnesium per day

Pre-pregnancy =
Pregnancy   = } 270mg
Breastfeeding = 320mg

TABLE 17
IRON CONTENT OF A SELECTION OF FOODS

	Description of serving	Weight	Iron Content per serving
STARCHY FOODS			
Bran Flakes	7 tablespoons	45g (1½oz)	9.0mg
All Bran	7 tablespoons	45g (1½oz)	5.4mg
Corn Flakes	6 tablespoons	35g (1¼oz)	2.3mg
Rice Krispies	9 tablespoons	35g (1¼oz)	2.3mg
Naan	1 naan	170g (6oz)	2.2mg
Pasta, wholemeal	6 tablespoons, cooked	150g (5¼oz)	2.1mg
Bread, wholemeal	2 slices, large loaf	75g (2¾oz)	2.0mg
Bread, white – high fibre	2 slices, large loaf	75g (2¾oz)	1.7mg
Chapati	1 (made without fat)	70g (2½oz)	1.6mg
Bread, white	2 slices, large loaf	75g (2¾oz)	1.2mg
Potato, jacket	1 large potato (with skin)	140g (5oz)	1.1mg
Oven chips	4 tablespoons	120g (4¼oz)	1.0mg
Pasta, white	6 tablespoons, cooked	150g (5¼oz)	0.8mg
VEGETABLES			
Spinach	2½ tablespoons, boiled	130g (4½oz)	5.2mg
Leeks	1 small leek, boiled	125g (4½oz)	2.5mg
Avocado pear	½ pear	130g (4½oz)	1.4mg
Beansprouts	1 cup	80g (2¾oz)	1.1mg
Peas, frozen	2½ tablespoons, boiled	75g (2¾oz)	1.1mg
Broccoli	2 spears, boiled	95g (3¼oz)	1.0mg
Spring greens	3 tablespoons, boiled	75g (2¾oz)	1.0mg
Radishes	4 radishes (raw)	50g (1¾oz)	1.0mg

	Description of serving	Weight	Iron Content per serving
FRUIT			
Figs, dried	4 figs	60g (2oz)	2.5mg
Apricots, dried	8 apricots	50g (1¾oz)	2.1mg
Prunes	8 prunes	40g (1½oz)	1.0mg
PROTEIN FOODS			
Kidney, lamb's	2 kidneys, fried	75g (2¾oz)	9.0mg
Lentils, green/brown	1 cup, cooked	150g (5¼oz)	5.2mg
Lentils, red	1 cup, cooked	150g (5¼oz)	3.6mg
Soya beans	4 tablespoons, cooked	105g (3¾oz)	3.2mg
Pilchards (in tomato sauce)	¼ large can	105g (3¾oz)	2.8mg
Baked beans	½ large tin	200g (7oz)	2.8mg
Red kidney beans	4 tablespoons, cooked	105g (3¾oz)	2.6mg
Red meat	2 thick slices, lean	85g (3oz)	2.4mg
Chick peas	4 tablespoons, cooked	105g (3¾oz)	2.2mg
Black-eye beans	4 tablespoons, cooked	105g (3¾oz)	2.0mg
Sunflower seeds	¼ cup	30g (1oz)	1.9mg
Kipper	2 fillets, baked	130g (4½oz)	1.8mg
Tofu	piece 2″ × 3″, steamed and fried	50g (1¾oz)	1.8mg
Cashew nuts	20 kernels	40g (1½oz)	1.5mg
Sesame seeds	sprinkling	15g (½oz)	1.2mg
Sausages	2 low-fat, grilled	90g (3oz)	1.2mg
Egg	1 size 2	60g (2oz)	1.1mg
Chicken	2 thick slices, breast	85g (3oz)	0.9mg
MISCELLANEOUS			
Cumin	2 teaspoons	10g	6.9mg
Thyme, dried	1 teaspoon	5g	6.2mg

	Description of serving	Weight	Iron Content per serving
Curry powder	2 teaspoons	10g	5.8mg

Recommended Nutrient Intake for Iron per day

Pre-pregnancy =
Pregnancy   = } 14.8mg
Breastfeeding =

TABLE 18
ZINC CONTENT OF A SELECTION OF FOODS

	Description of serving	Weight	Zinc Content per serving
STARCHY FOODS			
All Bran	7 tablespoons	45g (1½oz)	3.0mg
Bran Flakes	7 tablespoons	45g (1½oz)	1.5mg
Pasta, wholemeal	6 tablespoons, cooked	150g (5¼oz)	1.5mg
Naan	1 naan	170g (6oz)	1.4mg
Bread, wholemeal	2 slices, large loaf	75g (2¾oz)	1.3mg
Rice, brown/white	4 tablespoons, cooked	165g (5¾oz)	1.2mg
Pasta, white	6 tablespoons, cooked	150g (5¼oz)	0.7mg
Bread, white – high fibre	2 slices, large loaf	75g (2¾oz)	0.7mg
Chapati, non-fat	1 (made without fat)	70g (2½oz)	0.7mg
Potato, jacket	1 large potato (with skin)	140g (5oz)	0.7mg
Bread, white	2 slices, large loaf	75g (2¾oz)	0.4mg

	Description of serving	Weight	Zinc Content per serving
VEGETABLES			
Spinach	2½ tablespoons, boiled	130g (4½oz)	0.6mg
Peas, frozen	2½ tablespoons, boiled	75g (2¾oz)	0.5mg
Okra, fried	2½ tablespoons, stir-fried	50g (1¾oz)	0.5mg
Broccoli	2 spears, boiled	95g (3¼oz)	0.4mg
Cauliflower	10 florets, boiled	100g (3½oz)	0.4mg
PROTEIN FOODS			
Beef, lamb	2 thick slices, lean	85g (3oz)	4.6mg
Pork	1 chop	135g (4¾oz)	3.0mg
Cashew nuts	20 kernels	40g (1½oz)	2.2mg
Lentils, green/brown	1 cup, cooked	150g (5¼oz)	2.1mg
Sardines (in oil)	¾ can, drained	70g (2½oz)	2.0mg
Lentils, red	1 cup, cooked	150g (5¼oz)	1.5mg
Sunflower seeds	¼ cup	30g (1oz)	1.5mg
Chicken	2 thick slices, breast	85g (3oz)	1.3mg
Brazil nuts	9 kernels	30g (1oz)	1.3mg
Chick peas	4 tablespoons, cooked	105g (3¾oz)	1.2mg
Beans, various	4 tablespoons, cooked	105g (3¾oz)	1.0mg
Tofu	piece 2″ × 3″, steamed and fried	50g (1¾oz)	1.0mg
Tuna (in oil)	½ small can, drained	95g (3¼oz)	1.0mg
Egg	1 size 2	60g (2oz)	0.9mg
Peanuts	32 whole nuts	30g (1oz)	0.9mg
Sesame seeds	sprinkling	15g (½oz)	0.8mg
MILKS AND DAIRY FOODS			
Cheese, Cheddar-type	1 slice	40g (1½oz)	0.9mg
Cottage cheese	1 small carton	150g (5¼oz)	0.9mg
Milk (whole/skimmed)	⅓ pint	195g (7oz)	0.8mg

	Description of serving	Weight	Zinc Content per serving
Yoghurt, low-fat, fruit	1 small carton	150g (5¼oz)	0.7mg
Soya milk	⅓ pint	195g (7oz)	0.4mg

Recommended Nutrient Intake for Zinc per day

Pre-pregnancy = ⎱
Pregnancy = ⎰ 7.0mg
Breastfeeding (0–4 months) = 13.0mg
(4+ months) = 9.5mg

TABLE 19
COPPER CONTENT OF A SELECTION OF FOODS

	Description of serving	Weight	Copper Content per serving
STARCHY FOODS			
Rice, brown	4 tablespoons, cooked	165g (5¾oz)	0.54mg
Naan	1 naan	170g (6oz)	0.44mg
Muesli, no added sugar	6 tablespoons	95g (3¼oz)	0.32mg
Pasta, wholemeal	6 tablespoons, cooked	150g (5¼oz)	0.27mg
Oven chips	4 tablespoons	120g (4¼oz)	0.26mg
Rice, white	4 tablespoons, cooked	165g (5¾oz)	0.21mg
Sweet potato	2 medium, boiled	150g (5¼oz)	0.21mg
Potato, jacket	1 large potato (with skin)	140g (5oz)	0.20mg
Bread, wholemeal	2 slices, large loaf	75g (2¾oz)	0.20mg
All Bran	7 tablespoons	45g (1½oz)	0.20mg
Bran Flakes	7 tablespoons	45g (1½oz)	0.16mg

	Description of serving	Weight	Copper Content per serving
Pasta, white	6 tablespoons, cooked	150g (5¼oz)	0.15mg
Chapati	1 (made without fat)	70g (2½oz)	0.14mg
Pitta bread	1 pitta bread	65g (2¼oz)	0.14mg
Bread, white	2 slices, large loaf	75g (2¾oz)	0.14mg

VEGETABLES

Mushrooms	10 button mushrooms	55g (2oz)	0.22mg
Okra	2½ tablespoons, stir-fried	70g (2½oz)	0.13mg

FRUIT

Mango	1 mango (raw)	315g (11oz)	0.25mg
Guavas, tinned	6 halves	175g (6¼oz)	0.17mg
Lychees, tinned	10 lychees	150g (5¼oz)	0.16mg
Grapes (white/black)	small bunch	140g (5oz)	0.15mg
Pineapple, fresh	1 slice	125g (4½oz)	0.14mg
Raisins, sultanas	2 handfuls	35g (1¼oz)	0.14mg

PROTEIN FOODS

Cashew nuts	20 kernels	40g (1½oz)	0.80mg
Sunflower seeds	¼ cup	30g (1oz)	0.68mg
Brazil nuts	9 kernels	30g (1oz)	0.53mg
Lentils, green/brown	1 cup, cooked	150g (5¼oz)	0.50mg
Soya beans	4 tablespoons, cooked	105g (3¾oz)	0.34mg
Walnuts	9 halves	25g (1oz)	0.34mg
Hazelnuts	30 whole nuts	25g (1oz)	0.31mg
Peanuts	32 whole nuts	30g (1oz)	0.31mg
Tofu	piece 2″ × 3″, steamed and fried	50g (1¾oz)	0.29mg
Lentils, red	1 cup, cooked	150g (5¼oz)	0.29mg
Chick peas	4 tablespoons, cooked	105g (3¾oz)	0.29mg

	Description of serving	Weight	Copper Content per serving
Pork	2 thick slices, lean	85g (3oz)	0.25mg
Red kidney beans	4 tablespoons, cooked	105g (3¾oz)	0.24mg
Black-eye beans	4 tablespoons, cooked	105g (3¾oz)	0.23mg
Sesame seeds	sprinkling	15g (½oz)	0.22mg
Almonds	20 kernels	20g (¾oz)	0.20mg
Lamb	2 thick slices, lean	85g (3oz)	0.20mg
Pilchards (in tomato sauce)	¼ large can	105g (3¾oz)	0.20mg
Tuna (in oil)	½ small can, drained	95g (3¼oz)	0.19mg
Kipper	2 fillets, baked	130g (4½oz)	0.18mg
Sardines (in oil)	¾ can, drained	70g (2½oz)	0.13mg
Beef	2 thick slices, lean	85g (3oz)	0.12mg

Recommended Nutrient Intake for Copper per day

Pre-pregnancy = ⎫
Pregnancy   = ⎬ 1.2mg
Breastfeeding = 1.5mg

TABLE 20
IODINE CONTENT OF A SELECTION OF FOODS

	Description of serving	Weight	Iodine Content per serving
STARCHY FOODS			
Naan	1 naan	170g (6oz)	32mcg
Currant loaf	2 slices	75g (2¾oz)	22mcg
Hovis loaf	2 slices	75g (2¾oz)	17mcg

	Description of serving	Weight	Iodine Content per serving
Flour, white	4 tablespoons	100g (3½oz)	10mcg

―――――――――――――――― PROTEIN FOODS ――――――――――――――――

	Description of serving	Weight	Iodine Content per serving
Haddock	2 fillets, steamed	130g (4½oz)	247mcg
Cod	2 steaks, grilled	130g (4½oz)	143mcg
Kippers	2 fillets, baked	130g (4½oz)	91mcg
Salmon, red	½ small can	115g (4oz)	68mcg
Pilchards (in tomato sauce)	¼ large can	105g (3¾oz)	67mcg
Egg	1 size 1	60g (2oz)	32mcg

―――――――――――――――― MILKS AND DAIRY FOODS ――――――――――――――――

	Description of serving	Weight	Iodine Content per serving
Yoghurt, low-fast, fruit	1 small carton	150g (5¼oz)	72mcg
Milk (whole/skimmed)	⅓ pint	195g (7oz)	29mcg
Cheese, Cheddar-type	1 slice	40g (1½oz)	16mcg

―――――――――――――――― MISCELLANEOUS ――――――――――――――――

	Description of serving	Weight	Iodine Content per serving
Iodised salt	pinch	1g	310mcg
Salt, table	pinch	1g	4mcg

Recomended Nutrient Intake for Iodine per day

Pre-pregnancy =
Pregnancy   = } 140mcg
Breastfeeding =

TABLE 21
SELENIUM CONTENT OF A SELECTION OF FOODS

	Description of serving	Weight	Selenium Content per serving
STARCHY FOODS			
Naan	1 naan	170g (6oz)	43mcg
Bread, wholemeal	2 slices, large loaf	75g (2¾oz)	26mcg
Bread, white	2 slices, large loaf	75g (2¾oz)	21mcg
Rice, white	4 tablespoons, cooked	165g (5¾oz)	7mcg
VEGETABLES			
Mushrooms	10 button mushrooms, fried	55g (2oz)	7mcg
PROTEIN FOODS			
Brazil nuts	9 kernels	30g (1oz)	460mcg
Tuna (in oil)	½ small can, drained	95g (3¼oz)	86mcg
Kipper	2 fillets, baked	130g (4½oz)	65mcg
Lentils, green/brown	1 cup, cooked	150g (5¼oz)	60mcg
Plaice	2 small fillets, steamed	120g (4¼oz)	45mcg
Cod	2 steaks, grilled	130g (4½oz)	44mcg
Sardines (in oil)	¾ can, drained	70g (2½oz)	35mcg
Sunflower seeds	¼ cup	30g (1oz)	15mcg
Cashew nuts	20 kernels	40g (1½oz)	14mcg
Pork	2 thick slices, lean, roasted	85g (3oz)	12mcg
Egg	1 size 2	60g (2oz)	7mcg
Red kidney beans	4 tablespoons, cooked	105g (3¾oz)	6mcg

	Description of serving	Weight	Selenium Content per serving
MILKS AND DAIRY FOODS			
Cheese, Cheddar-type	1 slice	40g (1½oz)	5mcg

Recommended Nutrient Intake for Selenium per day

Pre-pregnancy = ⎫
Pregnancy   = ⎬ 60mcg
Breastfeeding = 75mcg

TABLE 22

ALCOHOL CONTENT OF ALCOHOLIC BEVERAGES

	Serving Size	Units per Serving
BEERS		
Beer	½ pint	1
	1 large can	1½
Lager	½ pint	1
	1 large can	1½
Pils-type lager	½ pint	2
	1 large can	3
Strong beer	½ pint	2
	1 large can	3
Guinness/stout	½ pint	1
Low alcohol beer/lager	½ pint	⅓
	1 pint	⅔
	1 can	½

	Serving Size	Units per Serving
CIDER		
Dry/sweet	½ pint	1
Diamond white	275ml bottle	2
Vintage	½ pint	3
WINE		
Red wine	1 standard wine glass	1
Rosé wine	1 standard wine glass	1
White wine	1 standard wine glass	1
Lower alcohol wine	1 standard wine glass	½
FORTIFIED WINE		
Port	pub measure	1
Sherry	pub measure	1
VERMOUTH		
Martini	pub measure	1
SPIRITS		
Whisky, gin, brandy etc.	pub measure	1

* Low alcohol beers, lagers, ciders and wines vary in alcohol content. Some contain about half as much alcohol as full strength varieties whilst others are virtually alcohol free – always check the label.

1 can = 16 fl oz = 440ml = ¾ pint

APPENDIX THREE

Useful Addresses

The following is a list of organizations which can be contacted for additional information, help or advice. Please enclose a stamped addressed envelope when applying.

Please note that all telephone numbers change from 16 April 1995. This means that all the 071s will be 0171; 081s will be 0181 and every other code (except for five places) will also take a 1 after the 0. Thus, 031 will be 0131; 041 will be 0141 and so on. The exceptions are Leeds, which changes from 0532 to 0113 with a 2 before the next digits; Sheffield, which changes from 0742 to 0114, with a 2 before the rest of the number; Nottingham changes from 0602 to 0115 with a 9 before the rest of the number; Leicester changes from 0533 to 0116 with a 2 before the next digits; and Bristol changes from 0272 to 0117 with a 9 before the rest of the number. You can still dial through on the old phone numbers until 16 April 1996. Conversely, you can use the new numbers as from 1 August 1994.

Action Against Allergy
43 The Downs
LONDON
SW20 8HS

Association of Breastfeeding Mothers
131 Mayou Road
LONDON
SE26 6EF

Tel: 0181 778 4769
0181 340 0470

Association for Improvements in the Maternity Services (AIMS)
Honorary Secretary
40 Kingswood Avenue
LONDON
NW6 6LS

Tel: 0181 778 0175

Association of Radical Midwives
Lakefield
8a The Drive
Wimbledon
LONDON
SW19

Association for Spina Bifida and Hydrocephalus (ASBAH)
ASBAH House
42 Park Road
PETERBOROUGH
PE1 2UQ

Tel: 01733 555988

Asthma Research Council
300 Upper Street
Islington
LONDON
N1 2XX

Tel: 0171 226 2260

British Diabetic Association
10 Queen Anne Street
LONDON
W1M 0BD

Tel: 0171 323 1531

British Dietetic Association
7th Floor
Elizabeth House
22 Suffolk Street
Queensway
BIRMINGHAM
B1 1LS

Tel: 0121 643 5483

British Nutrition Foundation
High Holborn House
52–54 High Holborn
LONDON
WC1V 6RU

Tel: 0171 404 6504

Coeliac Society
PO Box 220
HIGH WYCOMBE
Bucks
HP11 2HY

Tel: 01494 437278

Cystic Fibrosis Research Trust
5 Blyth Road
BROMLEY
Kent
BR1 3RS

Tel: 0181 464 7211

Department of Health Nutrition Unit
Wellington House
133–155 Waterloo Road
LONDON
SE1 8UG

Tel: 0171 972 2000

Eating Disorders Association
Sackville Place
44 Magdalen Street
NORWICH
Norfolk
NR3 1JU

Tel: 01603 621414

The Food Commission
102 Gloucester Place
LONDON
WC1

Tel: 0171 935 9078

Food Safety Advisory Centre
FOODLINE
PO Box 391
LONDON
WC1A 2PX

Tel: 0800 282407

Food Sense
(for publications from MAFF Food Safety Directorate)
LONDON
SE99 7TT

Tel: 0181 694 8862

Health Education Authority
Hamilton House
Mabledon Place
LONDON
WC1H 9TX

Tel: 0171 387 9528

Health Visitors Association
50 Southwark Street
LONDON
SE1 1UN

Tel: 0171 378 7255

La Leche League (Breastfeeding Support Group)
PO Box BM 3424
LONDON
WC1N 3XX

Tel: 0171 242 1278

Listeria Support Group
c/o Mark Horvath
Worlingworth
WOODBRIDGE
Suffolk
IP13 7NZ

Maternity Alliance (Campaign organization to improve pregnant women's rights)
59/61 Camden High Street
LONDON
NW1 7JL

Tel: 0171 837 1265

Migraine Trust
45 Great Ormond Street
LONDON
WC1N 3HD

Tel: 0171 278 2676

Ministry of Agriculture, Fisheries and Food (MAFF)
Nobel House
17 Smith Square
LONDON
SW1P 3HX

Tel: 0171 238 3000

Miscarriage Association
18 Stoneybrook Close
West Bretton
WAKEFIELD
West Yorks

Tel: 0192 485 515

National AIDS Helpline
Tel: 0800 567123

National Association for Colitis and Crohn's Disease (NACC)
98a London Road
ST ALBANS
Herts
AL1 1NX

The National Childbirth Trust
Alexandra House
Oldham Terrace
Acton
LONDON
W3 6NH

Tel: 0181 992 8637

National Eczema Society
Tavistock House East
Tavistock Square
LONDON
WC1H 9SR

Tel: 0171 388 4097

National Information for Parents of Premature Babies: Education, Resources and Support (NIPPERS)
49 Alison Road
Acton
LONDON
W3

Tel: 0181 992 9310

Nutrition Society
10 Cambridge Court
210 Shepherd's Bush Road
LONDON
W6 7NS

Tel: 0171 602 0228

Pre-Eclamptic Toxaemia Society
Ty Iago
High Street
LLANBERIS
LL55 4HB

Tel: 01286 872477

Slimming Magazine Clubs
Clubs Office
9 Kendrick Mews
Kensington
LONDON
SW7 3HG

Tel: 0171 225 1711

Soil Association Limited (Promotes organic food production)
86-88 Colston Street
BRISTOL
Avon
BS1 5BB

Tel: 0117 9290661

Twins and Multiple Birth Association
59 Sunnyside
WORKSOP
North Notts
S81 7LN

Tel: 01732 868000
    (6 pm–11 pm weekdays and at weekends)

The Toxoplasmosis Trust
Garden Studios
11–15 Betterton Street
LONDON
WC2H 9BP

Tel: 0171 713 0599

The Vegan Society
7 Battle Road
ST LEONARDS-ON-SEA
East Sussex
TN37 7AA

The Vegetarian Society
Parkdale
Dunham Road
ALTRINCHAM
Cheshire
WA14 4QG

Tel: 0161 928 0793

Weight Watchers
Kidwells Park House
Kidwells Park Drive
MAIDENHEAD
Berks
SL6 8YT

Tel: 01628 777077

WellBeing (Research charity to promote good health for women and babies)
Royal College of Obstetricians and Gynaecologists
27 Sussex Place
Regent's Park
LONDON
NW1 4SP

Tel: 0171 262 5337

Index